S0-BYY-429

Greenland

The End of the World

Damjan Končnik

Translation by Kevin Kato

BLUE FUJI

Greenland – The End of the World
Damjan Končnik & Kevin Kato
Published by Blue Fuji Publishers
Copyright © Damjan Končnik 2010

All rights reserved. No portion of this book may be reproduced, scanned or otherwise distributed in any electronic or printed form without the express written consent of the authors.

Cover Photos: Damjan Končnik
Cover Art: Kathy Aji
Translation/Edit: Kevin Kato

ISBN: 978-0-9843647-2-5
Library of Congress Control Number: 2010909820

For more information please contact the authors at:
damjankoncnik@gmail.com
kevin@kevinkato.com

Printed in the USA.
Simultaneously published in the UK.

Blue Fuji Publishers
East Hanover, New Jersey

For Mom & Dad

CONTENTS

FOREWORD

I met Damjan on a warm August evening, on the platform at the train station in Celje, Slovenia. This trip had been months in the making, and in that time I'd busied myself endeavoring, without much success, to tame the grammatical circus that is the Slovene language. Damjan spoke fair English, I knew, but at the very least an initial greeting in the local vernacular was in order.

He waved as I edged my annoying backpack (annoying to other people) through the light Sunday crowd. As I made it over to his spot on the cement I stuck out my hand – and my mind froze.

'...Hi, uh...Damjan...'

He chuckled and grabbed my hand.

'Kevin, welcome to Slovenia!'

And it was all English from there.

With a jubilant handshake and a pat on the arm Damjan's persona was easy to read: warm, friendly and thoroughly genuine. Within twenty minutes he was introducing me to the biggest pizza I'd ever seen, and we spent the next few hours chatting easily about our homes and our travels and my sweeping ignorance of Slovenia beyond the fact that the language is a very sick and cruel joke. (He agreed and apologized.) By the time we were washing down our last few bites with some exquisitely drinkable Laško beer (which I ordered successfully on my third try) I was seriously wondering if I hadn't somehow ended up with the wrong Damjan. This stout, easy-going guy picking leftover bits of cheese off the tray didn't exactly strike me as an adventurer. Not along the likes of Ernest Shackleton anyway.

But Damjan's story is not one of epic, world-class adventure. Yet it is an adventure still; an everyday odyssey of the mind, body and spirit.

We've all heard tales of the first men to journey to the South Pole; the first to scale the world's highest peaks; the first to fly across the ocean and around the world and to the moon. We hear these stories and, for a moment perhaps, dream of greatness for ourselves – and then we continue on with the normality of the day. Then there are those who traverse the Sahara on foot, cycle across Siberia, kayak from California to New Caledonia. *Crazy*, we think, shaking our heads. *Insane*. And in a way rightly so.

A story like Damjan's, however, gives us something else. A sense, maybe, that there are adventures for us too. Places. Pursuits. And in the dark corners of our souls, where we don't often look, vague ambitions begging to be let out into the light.

Damjan opened himself up and followed his ambitions, north to the end of the world. He faced solitude and uncertainty, stared down hardship and fate. Filled his eyes with immeasurable beauty while beating back visions of his own mortality.

And he came out on the other side a decidedly different person.

We may never ever feel the slightest desire to walk across Greenland alone, our immediate existence strapped to our backs.

But as Damjan says, 'Each one of us has a pole, an invisible force that spins the compass deep inside us, drawing us toward our dreams.' If we allow ourselves to follow this compass, wherever it points us, we too may become adventurers.

I hope you enjoy Damjan's tales as much as I've enjoyed trying to find the words to adequately relate them to you.

Tikilluarit Kalaallit Nunaat. Welcome to Greenland.

Kevin Kato

Preface

In the hills of northern Slovenia lies a little-known paradise called Vinska Gora. Awash in greenery, dotted with rocky outcroppings and laced with snaking rivers, 'Wine Mountain' (a regrettably dated name) presents as a bucolic prelude to Nature's grand stage. Here a young boy explores the world around him and develops a fascination – with geography, geology, biology, history, even chemistry and physics.

So it was for this geek in dirty boots, for Vinska Gora is my home.

Fast forward through the blur of my university years and a short-lived career in chemical technology, and here I am settling back into the shadow of the Kamniško-Savinjske Alps, in the land that bred my curiosities; the land that fed my wonder; the land that became my personal gateway to this beautiful, amazing planet.

My life as an explorer began under auspicious Spring skies as I packed up my backpack and set off for the far-flung corners of tiny Slovenia. I felt like a teenage Amundsen or

Scott, striking out to blaze new trails and discover new ground, seeking life and adventure in whatever form they might come. I marked my paths as I walked them. Stories piled up right along with my photographs. And my appetite for new lands outgrew my home. So I got a bigger bag and began crossing borders in search of other, foreign worlds.

I wandered the British Isles and dipped into Scandinavia, eventually immersing myself in the beauty of the scapes of Iceland. I ventured further overseas, crossing the varied expanses of the United States and then backtracking to visit the sands of Egypt. And though traveling in warmer climes comes with the allure of a much lighter load, I developed an affinity for cold and remote lands and in 2001 returned to the North Atlantic to set foot on the world's largest island.

In the course of my travels I couldn't say with certainty what I was looking for; the indefinable notions of adventure and freedom I suppose, along with some very tangible Viking ruins. But beyond these I didn't know what I was after.

Odd it was then when I realized I had found it.

I'm a hopeless lover of natural history; of sublime adventure; of the unspoiled majesty of the North. In the wilderness and along the roads that cut through, bringing me closer to the soul of the land, I feel alive. Alone, in small groups, among isolated communities, I find myself at home. Free from the habitual ligatures of civilization, I revel in the thought that I have arrived at the very end of the world. In this, there can be no place greater than Greenland.

For this is a land that charms and enchants; beckons and then broods; pulls you in with promise and then punishes you with her whims. Taking on this vast, wondrous island, one can not help but discover a world of adventure. Making peace with the land, one just may find contentment within himself.

Welcome to Greenland. I hope you enjoy the trip.

Damjan Končnik

Greenland

The End of the World

GREENLAND - THE END OF THE WORLD

DREAMS, SECRETS AND THE SELF

Quite unofficially, mountain climbing is the national sport of Slovenia. And straddling the invisible dotted line of the Arctic Circle, many official Slovenes can tell you, is a vast and rugged mountain climber's paradise. A curiously-named island of ice with gems yet to be discovered by most of the rest of the world, this remote land harbors an unfathomable wealth: of summits unconquered; of walls unclimbed; of plateaus awaiting their first encounter with man.

And gaping holes in the tundra and crevasses in the glaciers that can make your existence a thing of the past, but we'll get to that in due time.

The point is that the potential here is virtually unlimited, and poignantly unique. Where else on this entire planet can you name the mountain you've just climbed? (*Titan's Peak*, for example. *Heaven's Gate*. Or *Jeff*.) Where else can you seek out the priceless experience of becoming a part of climbing history? This is the underlying intrigue that draws alpinists and extreme adventure seekers to this land.

But what of the valleys, plains and fjords waiting quietly below?

I'd read somewhere that the lowlands of Greenland were equally captivating – a true trekking paradise for those who seek such places. But my imagination proved ill-equipped to fill in the blanks as to why. So off I went to the library and found, rather to my surprise, a couple of video documentaries about this intriguing island 'way up there.' What I saw when I flipped on my television were the expected fields of moss and lichens, rock-ridden hillsides, and an endless, snaking line separating the fantastically empty land and the freezing black-green Arctic waters. But mysterious Greenland, it soon became apparent, harbored so much more.

Who were the Vikings who sailed to this place more than a thousand years ago? In a world of possibilities, a good number of them tropical, why did they choose to settle in Greenland? And why did they then suddenly leave after five centuries of relative prosperity? How have the Inuit survived and sustained their ancient traditions in the face of the harsh Arctic climes?

The ghosts of history still lurked among the land.

The morning fog hung thick over the southern fringes of Greenland, refusing to rise as if daring me to come uncover her secrets. I imagined walking the land and stumbling upon some heretofore undiscovered Viking ruins, adding a page to the

Nordic story while carving out my own modest piece of Arctic history. This, for me, was the greatest lure of Greenland. This was the waking dream.

Years later, ensnared amidst the wide open nothingness, these aspirations would be wholly subsumed by much more mundane and urgent challenges – like finding firewood so I could eat.

When we hear the word trekking we might think of places like Nepal or Patagonia, where we wind toward our destination on well-marked paths. Porters stand by, ready to carry our bags, often with the help of horses or mules. Guides lead us, cooks cook for us, making sure we complete the journey comfortably and safely. With seasonal temperatures approaching twenty degrees, even at these latitudes and altitudes, we can be assured of agreeable warmth; if it does rain, or if the cold sets in, we can usually find quick shelter in a lodge or tea shop.

So what can be expected in a place like Greenland, eighty percent buried under a blanket of ice? The weather across the island is fairly stable; much of the precipitation is confined to the south, driving most adventurers toward the drier, more agreeable north. But wherever you go, marked paths are scarce. Professional guides are unheard of. You are alone, left to your own devices. You put your pack on your own back and you blaze your own trail.

Only a few hundred people a year venture off in this land of ice and isolation, with nothing but a map and their orientation skills to guide them. Greenland's proximity to magnetic north, itself not an unwavering constant, adds directional declination to the mix and furthers the challenge. Trekking in Greenland also means a date with permafrost. While the ground on top can be anywhere from damp to downright soggy, underneath lies an eternally frozen world. Weak ankles and light sleepers need not apply.

The challenges demand we approach with intelligence, proper equipment and boundless self-sufficience. But trekking in the Arctic requires more than physical and practical agility. You must be ready to face ice-cold rivers and streams; to find your way in a thick fog; to stare down thoughts of danger; to defeat solitude and isolation; to go potty in the grass. You must understand that if something goes wrong, perhaps no one will ever know. You are utterly alone. Alone to draw and conquer your own frontiers (and dig your own latrine).

Yet Greenland offers innumerable paths to those willing to seek them out. And her vast dimensions are magnificent. Witnessing the earth-shaping strength of glaciers; watching bergs and ice floes slip silently past your feet; walking among unnamed rivers, lakes and summits; basking in the soft glow of the midnight sun; feeling yourself being drawn to treat more gently the flora and fauna that surround you – this is the magic, and the reward, of the challenge.

For this novice trekker, Greenland also offers exceptional photographic opportunities. Visibility in the clean, cold air will sometimes extend two or perhaps three hundred kilometers. If conditions along the eastern coast are right, you can actually see Iceland floating on the distant horizon.

Yes, the beauty to be captured is immeasurable. And the land itself is the treasure. For this is a country with no high pyramids, no large temples, no wide fortifications or mighty castles, as the native Inuit were immersed in more basic, life-sustaining pursuits. The singular great achievement of which the first inhabitants of Greenland can boast is having survived five thousand arctic winters intact – a monument of the spirit, exceptional, perhaps, as any pile of stone.

Though I would travel this land alone, I wanted to find a soul mate to walk with me, someone who had already lived the adventure and could share his nurtured spirit. I searched the web and found a man named Clemens, who two years previous had trekked solo to a place called Paradisdalen, the 'Paradise Valley.' We agreed to meet in Vienna, and for two days I drank in rousing stories of his adventures.

The glacial river was absolutely exploding,' he said, able to laugh now. *'If someone on that ship hadn't seen my signal rocket I might never have made it back to camp or seen my darling Vienna again!'*

I'll concede I was a bit unnerved.

Rivers can rise quickly during the warm summer season, Clemens went on to explain, becoming impassable torrents, twenty, thirty, sometimes forty meters wide or more. A subtle warning, I supposed, of what my own future might hold. But his photographs of Paradise Valley overrode whatever dangers Greenland might present.

I knew of the magic of the cold colors of the North, but

gazing at the gentle strength of the orange light coming through in his pictures was like looking at my first girlie magazine. This was unlike anything I'd ever seen before. And almost without knowing why, I knew I had to experience it all for myself.

Back on the train, heading for Slovenia and home, I hadn't a shred of doubt left in my mind.

I would go.

I would walk toward the far polar reaches. I would face what trials and crises and crevasses awaited. I would immerse myself in the magic of desolation. I would sleep in wide empty spaces and avail my soul to the secrets, silences and solitude of this land.

And, with any luck, there at the end of the world, I would discover these things in myself.

IN SEARCH OF PARADISE

FIRST TRIP TO GREENLAND, 2001

In 1972 brothers Hans and Jokum Gronvold were out hunting on the Nuussuaq Peninsula in western Greenland when they came upon a pile of rocks. Not just a heap of rocks but a neat or at the very least not wholly natural arrangement. Drawn in by their curiosity, the brothers began turning them aside – and discovered a grave containing the frozen remains of eight women and children. It may be misleading to use the word remains, however, as their seal skin clad bodies were so efficiently mummified by the frigid climate that five hundred years after their burial, tattooed lines could still be seen on the women's faces.

I stared at the map spread out across my kitchen table and thought about getting my parents' phone number tattooed on my forearm, just in case.

My finger seemed to move of its own free will, following the rows of crosses marking the ruins and remains of the Vikings who occupied southern Greenland a millenium ago. Treks and tracks abound on the world's largest island, but my sights were set on the southern Qaqortoq Peninsula, center of medieval activity and life on this cold green land. Here I would find, among half-buried bits of fable and history, the best-preserved Viking ruin on the island, the sacred stones of Hvalsey Church. (The Waikiki Hilton just doesn't do it for me, what can I say?)

Tracing lines and circles across the page, I could feel the cold breath of the ghosts of history on my fingertips. This alone was enough to draw me to the isolated southern extremes of this very north-lying island.

But Qaqortoq boasted more than just scattered remnants of man. Nature also stated her rugged case here, in the form of fjords and glaciers and a land thick with detail. I found myself pondering a day's detour north to the dark waters of forbidding Lake Motzfeld, set among some of the area's most beautiful and treacherous terrain. As I ran my eyes across the land, drinking in the possibilities, into my head drifted the comically upbeat voice of Niels, a travel agent from Copenhagen and a man of many tales who had spent one glorious arctic summer in Qaqortoq.

'*This one route leads to a magnificent glacier,*' he explained. '*You'll find some of the most breathtaking views of the lake here...*'

I imagined myself standing on the precipice of the greatest garden on Earth.

'*... as long as you avoid the crevasses along the way.*'

And stepping into my very own tomb of ice and snow.

Niels continued to breezily describe the juxtaposition of

beauty and death he was walking me into, and I wondered aloud if there wasn't someone who could accompany me on this side trek. I'm all for adventure, but I wasn't so keen on the tattoo idea. Niels said he'd look into it – then picked up a pencil and asked for my parents' phone number.

But lifeguard or not, I had no doubts as to what lay ahead of me: The trek of a lifetime. And a true arctic paradise. Honestly, I couldn't wait.

To round out the experience I wanted to walk among the surviving traditions of Greenland's native people. They most certainly weren't still living in igloos (were they?), but how to find out what life was presently like at the far reaches of the world? One possibility would be to visit Aappilattoq, a very special village in a very special place among the vast expanses of Greenland, or so the story went. Journeying to this far-flung community would be a treasure in itself; the trip would take me through venerable Torssukatak Fjord, a narrow waterway hemmed in by towering mountains of gray and black (and perhaps not falling) rock. After a stop in the village to taste the life of the modern Inuit I could set off for the wild once more, to seek out evidence of the life of the first people to set foot on this green and icy world.

I felt warm, like when I drink coffee too fast, as I imagined navigating my solitary way across the Qaqortoq wilderness; cruising along the desolation of the south coast; reaching my ultimate destination, Aappilattoq, for a few days of more relaxing exploration before going off to seek out the ghosts of Greenland's heritage. But what would I find out there among the furthest fringes of paradise? Would anyone there speak my language? Would I even be welcome? Where would I go from this tiny community, squeezed in between deep fjords and high mountains, to discover the remnants of history still lurking nearby? *How* would I go?

Through the rumble of questions in my head I heard a faint voice of inspiration, assuring me I'd find someone I could convince to take me to some of the places where the Inuit used to live. Places where they'd once slept and survived in sealskin tents. Where I could rest my hands on their tell-tale circles of rocks. Where I could discover unnamed lakes and waterfalls; track down colonies of fat, barking seals; gaze upon glaciers that stretched down from the mountains into dark emerald fjords. All while not stepping into a crevasse.

The pagan gods were smiling on me; Niels told me he knew a hunter who could show me the age-old spirit of this village at the end of the world. A few more emails back and forth put some meat on my skeletal plans, and as sure as a whale's got blubber I knew Aappilattoq was going to add a lot of spice to an already appetizing adventure. Further beefing up my itinerary I decided on a couple days in the village of Nanortalik; then a helicopter drop in trekking distance of Qassiarsuk, where stands a house built by Erik the Red, the first Viking to set foot on southern Greenland. From there a hike to Tasiusaq, a hamlet on the edge of the Sermilik Ice Fjord, followed by a sweep through a neighboring valley to seek out a roaring, pounding, almost mythical waterfall with no name. This final quest fulfilled, I would be ready to head back to Narsarsuaq and civilization.

I outlined my plans to Niels, who warned me straight away that such a trek was inordinately ambitious if not outright unachievable. Aside from certain niggling legalities regarding trekking in the Arctic and sub-Arctic (to keep novice trekkers from adding to the mummy count), I needed to consider just how far I could walk in one day with thirty kilograms of gear on my back. Conventional trekking wisdom, he explained, says a comfortable day's walk ceases to be so after around twenty-seven kilometers. If you aren't familiar with the area and the path is not marked, deduct two to five kilometers. Subtract another three to five if the trail involves any long, demanding ascents. On top of this I would factor in a couple of extra days for rest or for correcting any logistical setbacks, as well as for moving at my own definition of comfortable. Plus I'd have to respect the weather. The dry Arctic climate does not apply in southern Greenland, where more than 2500 millimeters of precipitation falls annually – almost as much as in the Alpine region of Europe.

I reminded myself, as did Niels (more than once), that this would be my first trip to this vast, empty island. But I decided to stick to my original course – though I'd keep a few shorter versions in my back pocket. I would also read up a little more on the ins and outs of the area – or should I say the ups and downs and long acrosses. But I wasn't going to spend valuable preparation time gobbling up stacks of literature. Physical and psychological readiness was what would ultimately get me through. This, at least, was my hope.

11

My foggy Arctic dreams were crystallizing. I would point my compass north and follow in the footsteps of those who first came this way over a thousand years ago. Granted, my Viking brethren hadn't the means to google ahead to ready themselves for their journey. They didn't have a haphazard stack of maps to help guide them as I did. I'd wear Gore-tex, not sheepskin. I'd arrive by plane. Still, once my boots landed I would be walking across the same glaciers and green pastures they had. I would gaze out over the same icy lakes and grand fjords that they saw. And I would seek out the provident life of the Inuit that had barely changed since the Vikings discovered this land ten centuries before me.

Whales do indeed have blubber. This was going to be good.

THE ROAD TO COPENHAGEN

The final hour had arrived. I pushed myself away from my desk as the clock struck lunch and headed for home and Greenland. Marko, my co-worker from the ecological institute, sped along behind me and sat quietly in my kitchen, gazing around as I wolfed down some leftovers and sucked down two cups of my favorite Turkish coffee. I gave the dishes a rough washing as he mumbled something about my rucksack, packed tight with clothes, cookware, dry food, camera, film, tent and anything else I thought I might need to survive and to live. He looked up as I turned around, dishes done.

  'No room for the dog sled, Damjan?...'

Leaving my car and my life as I knew it in Vinska Gora, I rode with Marko to the Celje train station. *'Best of luck,'* he said, shaking my hand like it was our last. I slapped him on the shoulder. 'I'm going to Greenland, not to war. See you in a few weeks.'

As he disappeared behind the swinging station doors the feeling hit me.

I was alone.

I leaned my pack against a pole. The clock above read 1:30. I paced to the end of the platform and back, to the end and back, three times. Images of bleak, desolate tundra sat quiet and heavy in my head. I checked the clock again. 1:35. Time, it seemed, would crawl until I got on that train.

If not for work I could have taken the direct morning line and done my waiting in Vienna. Still, jumping the 2:00 would put me in Vienna with enough time to catch the overnight bus to Copenhagen – assuming I made my one and only connection in Bruck an der Mur...

The graceful Austrian countryside couldn't pass by quickly enough as the minutes sped by. By the time we were clacking into Bruck an der Mur my lifeline to Vienna was already there, unnerving in its calm resemblance to a train ready to roll. I ran (an extremely generous description) for the end of the car, my pack bouncing and skidding along the narrow corridor walls. I exploded out the door and onto the platform – and the squeeze bottle in my pack's side pocket went flying and tumbling down onto the tracks. I looked down. I glanced over at my lifeline. I

13

looked down at my bottle again. I was about to chalk up my first loss of the trip when a man with a lot more time on his hands than me – and plenty more agility in his unladen frame – calmly reached down and picked it up. 'Danke!' I huffed as I stumbled off, my pack as accommodating as a suit of armor.

I crashed through the folding doors as the conductor was blowing his whistle, a breathless *Gott sei Dank!* falling out of my mouth. I shouldered my way down another narrow corridor and plopped into an empty seat, no room for my pack except out in the passageway. A procession of passengers grumbled in German as they maneuvered their own bulky selves past and over, one of them cursing out loud the owner of this ill-placed pack sitting silently by.

The ride to Vienna gave me a chance to collect my breath and my wits. Upon arrival the chase resumed as I had barely an hour to catch a bus to the international bus terminal, pay for the ticket I'd reserved, find the right bus among the crowds and announcements and exhaust and get my butt on board for the overnight trip through the Czech Republic to Berlin. Safely settled into my seat, I still couldn't look forward to a nice, quiet, uninterrupted ride; traveling through the Czech Republic in 2001 meant a passport check, the only one along the entire route through to Germany and on into Denmark and all the way to Greenland. Not that passport checks are cause for alarm, but it was one more nuisance to crowd my head as my journey took me slowly, steadily northward. That and the sudden worry there was no toilet on board.

There was, and after a quick visit I could finally start to

relax. Dreary announcements about all things *verboten* drifted in and out of my consciousness. The passport control officers at the Czech border moved with an air of leftover communist-era disdain; I wasn't sure I was happy about being fully awake for them or not. I dozed on and off the rest of the way to Berlin, where I would transfer to the final leg of my overland journey. Stretching my legs out on the plush Danish bus that would carry me the rest of the way to Copenhagen, I felt good. I felt relaxed. I was on track. Even the driver's voice came across as a gentle breeze after the stern gusts of instruction our German Fahrer had been whipping at us.

We arrived in Copenhagen around three o'clock, a smidgen behind schedule but with no more bus transfers to make what did it matter? I'd made it through the first part of my journey with my mind, my itinerary and my supply of water bottles intact. I strolled away from the bus, in high spirits about things both behind and ahead.

Then came Tina.

A representative of the local Greenland Travel office, she was waiting at the bus station with an envelope fat with airline tickets, accommodation vouchers, ship chits and helicopter transport papers. *'I was afraid something would get lost in the mail,'* she explained as she handed it all over, a look in her eye like it had happened before. What I didn't realize until later was her notion of war in the region around Slovenia, of rockets flying, disrupting the safe delivery of my documents. Silly girl.

'So how are you holding up?' she asked. I glanced over her silky features. She looked rather Asian, as Inuit often do. 'Well,

let me just say it's good to be here,' I said, a dimwitted smile on my face I'm sure. Then, offering reports of the cloudy, rainy weather waiting for me in the south of Greenland, she wished me a pleasant journey. It wasn't until I had my bags and half my body in a taxi when out of nowhere she suggested doing something in town together, later that evening. I studied her innocent expression again. *Did she always meet her clients at the bus station to pass papers and make passes?* The fantasies started flooding my head and I told myself unequivocally that I was just another client and she was just a nice person and I needed some rest to mitigate the sleep-deprivation that was already and quite clearly affecting my judgment.

In the cab I kidded myself into believing that if I'd said yes I never would have made it to Greenland.

I fell onto my bed, wanting only sleep after an eighteen-hour bus trip. But thoughts of tomorrow and Greenland and Tina and my waning hours in Copenhagen left me staring at the gray hostel ceiling.

I slid out of bed ahead of my alarm, blessedly rejuvenated. I don't know when I finally slipped off, but once I did that was it. Nothing but the black of another dreamless sleep. An hour later, all packed up and a thick bread-heavy breakfast in my gut, I was hailing a taxi and heading for the airport. Nothing now but a simple plane ride separated me from Greenland.

At check-in I ruffled through my pack one final time to make sure I had everything. I certainly did – and then some, it seemed. The combination scale and conveyor belt (I have no idea how these two can be combined) said my pack weighed two kilograms more than when I weighed him fully-loaded at home. *How do these things happen?* Did Marko pack me some Turkish coffee back in Vinska Gora? Food for the sled dogs? Was Tina hiding in there? She *was* rather petite. I also had too much hand luggage according to the regulations the check-in girl was reciting to me. And I wasn't the only scofflaw. Three others – a trio of German climbers – also had overweight packs. The girl's blank reaction told me she'd been through this before. In time we were forgiven and asked to wait for our boarding call.

In those minutes I looked around, taking in the group of passengers who would make up our half-empty flight. Besides the Germans were a small group of fishermen and two cuddly pairs of trekkers. The rest appeared to be local Greenlanders or Danish retirees, off for a bit of rest and relaxation on one of the coldest islands on Earth.

The feeling I had at Celje Station rushed back into my gut.

I would be on my own in paradise.

KALAALLIT NUNAAT – LAND OF (NO) PEOPLE

I shifted around as much as my narrow seat would allow, giddy with anticipation of watching Greenland come creeping over the horizon. The woman next to me was slapping her hands on her armrests, clearing her throat, wheezing like a cat choking on its own furball – an obvious and vaguely nauseating attempt at telling me to stop hogging the window. I shifted again and pressed my forehead against the glass. For nothing as it turned out, as a fat blanket of cloud cover had already taken care of any chance at a view of the land. I looked at the woman and shrugged. 'Not much to see.' She shot me an ornery glance and leaned over my lap, stretching her neck like one of those Paduang women and peering out at the expanse of gray below us. 'So I see,' she muttered, and settled back in her seat, eyeing me like it was my fault.

We (meaning I) did catch a glimpse of fabled Erik the Red country as we descended toward Narsarsuaq, the 'Great Plain'. The blue-black sea below appeared both calm and voracious – like a pair of scaly nostrils swimming a slow line in the general direction of your rowboat. Our plane pitched and dipped, in no unusual manner but a bit too much for my liking. I held my breath. The hungry water closed in - then in the blink of an eye disappeared, replaced with the gray-brown blur of the land. A jolt and a rumble and the roar of a plane pushing the limits of luck and physics. I pushed back against my seat. I hate this part. We bounced and lurched and finally slowed. I let my breath out and smiled at my neighbor, tossing a thumb at the window. She frowned and looked away.

Only later would I notice the knuckled mountains of rock, snow and ice rising up from the far end of the runway, waiting to chew up any aircraft that strayed past the end of the short strip of more or less ice-free macadam. In retrospect I figured that old woman should be thanking me for sparing her the visual terror.

I stepped off the plane and sucked in my first lungful of the clean, cold Greenland air. I felt like I was being cleansed, body and soul. Then I walked through the glass doors of the terminal and into swirls of cigarette smoke so thick I could barely make out the oversized 'No Smoking' sign on the wall. Only the high ceilings kept us all from slowly succumbing to this unusual Inuit welcome – and a not-so-subtle hint about the attitude of the natives. That sign was for the Danes and anyone else who invaded this land; the Inuit were free to do however they damn well pleased.

In the slightly fresher arrival hall a woman materialized in front of me. *'I am Judu,'* she said, offering her hand. *'From the Danish travel agency in Narsarsuaq.'* She tossed me a demure smile. *'Would you like me to walk you to the hostel?'*

I adjusted my pack. I liked Greenland already. 'No, that's all right. Just point me in the right direction.'

Ten minutes later I exited the airport and headed off in the wrong direction.

After a suspiciously long stretch of gravel and crumbling pavement I walked into the only building around resembling a youth hostel. Next thing I knew I was in a hotel bar, standing next to a carved polar bear, talking to a guy named Jörg.

'Where you going with that big pack?' he asked between mouthfuls of beer. I pulled out a map and traced the route I had laid out for myself, sliding my finger past ferry jumps and fjords to my ultimate destination: Aappilattoq, population 160. *'Oh, that's where my fiancée lives,'* he said, grabbing my shoulder. *'You'll have to come visit us while you're in town.'*

As if it meant going out of my way.

The weather wasn't extending a very cheerful welcome, but I was quickly feeling part of the local community. Jörg gave Judu a quick call (I suppose I shouldn't have been surprised they knew each other) and barely had time to throw the rest of his beer down his throat before she was pulling up in front of the hotel to whisk us half a mile down the street, past the airport and to the hostel. Judu's travel agency owned the place so she was there quite often, assisting guests in whatever capacity. Jörg seemed a sort of drifter who hung out at the hostel for lack of any better place to be. I paused for a moment, taking in my perfectly disorganized introduction to Greenland.

In a room with a bed for only the second time in what seemed like a week, I dropped my pack and kicked off my boots and stretched myself out. But the thought quickly sank in: *What a witless waste of time!* So I pulled my boots back on and headed for Blomsterdalen, the Valley of Flowers, and a view of nearby Kuussuup Glacier.

Blomsterdalen was appropriately blooming, a kaleidoscope of color splashed over a canvas of moss and creeping white lichens. Small patches of twiggy, leafy scrub dotted the gently rolling hills. The land looked entirely untended yet wonderfully tame. The misty weather, hanging like a curtain in the distance, blotted out not only the glacier I had come to see but the million broken-toothed mountains that I knew were waiting for me out there.

For the moment, it was easy to imagine Greenland as a kind, forgiving host.

Growing all around and right at my feet even were clumps of wild blueberries, cool and sweet as ice cream. Already I was feeling like a true explorer, surviving off the land I walked upon. I also stumbled across some wild mushrooms, not the perfect compliment to blueberries but an adventurer in the wild can't be picky. I picked a few and held them in my hand. Earlier, considering the possibility of getting lost and having to forage the land to survive (this brought on by my not being able to find the hostel in a half-mile radius) I had asked Judu about the native wild plants. She assured me the mushrooms were not the kind to turn my trek into a visit to Wonderland. So I put a few in my pocket.

I was pushing the last of my blueberries into my mouth as I strolled into the common area back at the hostel. Like a bunch of starving marmots the other guests in the room came up and started pawing me. 'They're a bit on the sour side,' I lied through a puddle of blueberry juice. Their expressions went from mild disappointment (*Darn, they looked really good.*) to knowing relief (*Well we don't want to get sick, do we?*) to cock-eyed suspicion (*Hey so why are you filling your face with them then?!*).

I swallowed loud and hard, feeling vaguely guilty about trying to keep the world's largest island all to myself. So I went back out and gathered up a fresh handful to share with anyone wanting to try. 'Here, I found some sweeter ones.' (*Funny, they look just like the sour ones. What's your name again?...*) One older woman from Canada was especially tickled to be tasting '*the real, wild Greenland.*' Jörg eyed her as she chatted through bits of blueberry, trying to figure out for his own odd suspicions where she was really from. *'I bet she's Japanese,'* he muttered over my shoulder, leaving me to figure out why it might matter. Three more people then asked me where they could go to get some for themselves and hurried off into the damp, chilly evening.

I turned to Jörg and asked him if he was interested in trying a little soup made with fresh Greenland mushrooms – a sort of thank-you for inviting me to spend some time with him and his fiancée though I had my doubts anything would come of it. He looked at me, a haze of distrust in his eyes. So I pulled a mushroom out of my pocket and tossed it into my mouth, smiling as I chomped away.

His eyes lit up, and in the next second he was off scrounging up potatoes and bowls and everything else we needed for a steaming pot of home-made, warm-the-bones mushroom soup.

When we sat down, Jörg's suspicious leer returned. I'd scarfed down half my bowl before he'd taken his first bite. 'I'll eat it if you don't want it,' I said through a mouthful of potatoes. A guy named Jörg, I thought, should not be nervous about a bowl of soup. He dipped his spoon and took a hesitant sip. After that his arm didn't stop moving until his bowl was empty. *'Damn, that was good,'* he said between swigs from a bottle of vodka in the staff refrigerator. Judu suddenly appeared. *'You shouldn't be drinking that.'* She narrowed her eyes and shook her head and floated back out the door.

I went for more soup and Jörg fell into an unsolicited explanation about how he was supposed to go to Aappilattoq that day, but the night before he'd ended up in bed with a local lady. Only the sound of his helicopter taking off for Nanortalik had woken him up. *'Good soup,'* he added, and walked out of the room.

I fired up a batch of rice for the morning, noticing the clock on the wall. It was barely eight o'clock but my internal chimes were striking midnight. I cleaned up the last few stray dishes and hit the sack – and tossed and turned for an hour and a half before my hectic visions of the next ten days finally blurred and faded.

A 4pm ferry across the fjord to Ittleq the next day afforded me the satisfying luxury of sleeping in as long as I wanted. But after years of daydreaming about this trip how could I spend my first morning in bed? After one final equipment check and a quick look around a Jörg-less hostel I went out to track down some gas for my burner; then the requisite stop in the tourist office to get the local version of the path that lay ahead. From Ittleq it would be a short walk to Igaliku; then a hike up to and along the Black River to that glacier-fed beauty called Lake Motzfeld. If conditions were right I'd have time to make a pass along the southern edge of the lake and have adequate fuel, food and time to get me down to Qaqortoq. But a check on the weather forecast put a quick and sure end to all that. After a day of sun the clouds would move back in, and a very wet, foggy spell was expected. The guy asked me if I wanted a printout of the forecast – to remind me of the weather as if it weren't going to be dripping all over me anyway. I thanked him and tossed my visions of Motzfeld in the can.

Back at the hostel I told Judu of my quickly-disintegrating plans. She'd probably heard the same self-pitying crap from a hundred trekkers before me but I pressed on. Either to ease my pain or shut me up she told me to leave my rucksack with her; she'd bring it down to the ferry dock for me later. So with only a light daypack on my back I set off on a wandering walk around Narsarsuaq.

The Narsarsuaq airport, or at least the runway, was built by the US military in 1941. The town only existed then to serve the airport, and has managed to retain its original lack of charm. The one sight, so to speak, is a fireplace left standing after a hospital at the northeast edge of town burned down. There is also the modest Signal Hill, from where one can enjoy a view of the fjord. Overall, it came as no surprise I'd end up at the pier an hour early.

The winds were blowing chunks of blue-white ice into the bay, packing them in tight enough to allow for a jaunty walk around on the water (which doesn't seem like a healthy idea but if the polar bears can do it so can I.) The ice was comprised of several layers reflecting various shades of light, testifying to their differing ages and qualities. Greenland, I could see, had a million secrets to tell. I watched yesterday's group of German trekkers push off toward the mountains. *Among some of the most beautiful on our plane*t I heard one say. I silently wished them luck and headed back across the ice and toward the docks.

The ferry's first stop was on the far side of the fjord at sleepy

Qassiarsuk, which by Greenland standards is firmly within the realm of civilization. Next up was Ittleq, boasting Greenland's largest sheep farm and a total human population of one. I wondered how often that one person needed a ferry as I hopped off. As the boat pushed away everyone started waving good-bye, though not in that cheerful 'have a good time' way; it was more like a 'good luck you're gonna need it pal' sort of send-off. I waved back as they floated off into the gray distance.

The route from Ittleq, leading through rolling green fields, up over a modest ridge and down to the town of Igaliku, is known as the Royal Way. *What an appetizing moniker for the first leg of my journey*, I thought. And a fitting title on its own, the land breathing with an almost magnanimous air. Standing at the vast entrance to my Greenlandic adventure, I couldn't imagine a more beautiful setting for taking my first real steps.

Thoughts like these help – marginally, but they help – when you are carrying thirty-three kilograms of gear on your back for the first time.

I strapped my day bag to my rucksack and held the monster at my feet. He felt heavy but balanced. I checked my map, positioned my compass, and calculated in my head an extra degree of deviation. It was time to go, I knew.

I lifted my pack onto my shoulders. After all the preparation, both physical and mental, I was now standing at the starting line. The beginning would be the most difficult part. The entire long trek lay ahead. But of course, traveling even the longest road begins with one step. The way is a bit less formidable with a goal to aim for. Will sets you in motion and keeps you going.

Persistence and determination mitigate long paths and harsh weather. And, maybe, leaden rucksacks. Holy cow.

The landscape spread out all around me, presenting faces of nature I'd never seen: icebergs playing in slow-motion along the rough edges of the fjord; mowed fields pushing against wild meadows; mountains jutting from the water's edge sixteen hundred meters into the sky; distant glaciers spilling into the valleys; fields of (oddly enough, I thought) potatoes; swamps, lakes and sheep, and isolated farms scattered far and wide. The ground rose slowly, inviting me to slow down and take it all in. I felt light, as if I were walking in a dream, until I crested a hill and spotted Igaliku sitting sleepily at the edge of a narrow fjord. In the distance, Narsarsuk Mountain (not to be confused with Narsarsuaq the town) rose like a castle in a tellurian fairytale. The view, I could say, was enough to take my breath away. I'll admit though that it was this initial walk that had me sucking on the sub-Arctic breezes. This plus spending a half hour trying to nail down the elusive correct pronunciation of the village's name. *Ee-YEH-lee-ko, Damjan, Ee-YEH-lee-ko!* I could still hear Jörg saying as he wiped more mushroom soup off his chin with his sleeve.

Approaching the modest settlement brought me my first real encounter with the locals, busy out in the sloping fields gathering sunbeams and soaking up the scenery. *Sunbathing in Greenland*, I mused. This was definitely not Waikiki. I plodded down to the village skirts where I came across what might have been half the population of the town gathered around a large cow-milking apparatus. Folks old and young were standing in a half-circle watching a man with a very intense expression milk a stocky black number who didn't look nearly as interested as everyone else. So engrossed were all these people (and who could blame them?) they didn't notice the sweaty pale-skinned guy with the huge rucksack standing among them.

After two hours hiking across postcard-perfect landscapes, my Greenland adventure, I felt, had finally, truly begun.

Eminently satisfied with the cow-milking exhibit I headed straight for the hills on the far side of town. This based on my assumption (okay, my wild hope) that if my legs were going to give out it would be around the fifth day, not the first. Shuffling around town today would only increase my odds of collapsing in a heap all alone out in no-man's land a few days later. And of course, I'd much rather collapse in a heap when there are other human beings around. So I'd get on my way, get this first leg of the trek under my belt and check out town (and collapse in a heap) when I made it back.

Out just past the other side of town I encountered my first glacial river. This is exciting stuff for a nascent trekker, and by nascent I mean stupid enough to get excited about an ice-cold river in my way. This being Greenland, I wanted to know not what the river was named so much as if it had a name at all. Looking around, I then began to wonder if anyone had ever been to the other side. Up into the mountains and all the way down to the water there was nary a sign of a viable crossing – no bridge, no planks, not even a stepping stone. Zero. Zilch.

Not that there was much for the locals to cross over to.

Now, there are certain things, at home or in the office, that I can always find when I need them; a pen or a rubber band, for example. A paper clip. A roll of tape (though not always with tape). But out here? I needed either a bridge or a jet pack, neither of which I'd ever seen at home or work so what hope did I have? Yet there she was, an old gate, lying in the grass, nothing like a fence or anything else around that might require a gate. So it was fair game as far as I was concerned. Tickled at my odd luck, I dragged my bridge to the river's edge, stood it on end and let it fall down over the rushing waters. Then I stood back and watched it get tossed like a leaf downstream. Luckily it didn't get far, as it got wedged into such a position where it would serve quite well, though not as a bridge so much as the plank on a pirate ship.

I stuck my fingers into the ice-cold river.

Never cross barefoot goes the adage, as your feet are quite likely to find all manner of slick plant life and razor-sharp rocks waiting in ambush beneath the surface. I glanced over at my gate, a preternatural sensation of my head being cracked open coming over me. I took off my boots and threw on my spare pair of shoes.

I hadn't even gotten my second foot in when it was already obvious: the river wanted nothing but to pull me and my pack right down into the arctic underworld. The water was only up to my knees, but felt strong enough to knock a pack mule right off its four feet. And as I had only half that many the river took a terrifying eternity to ford. The next wet march of doom, another hour ahead, I was able to conquer in only about half of forever. And thus I began building up my confidence as a trekker in the wilderness, with or without gates or bridges.

My first of many late evening dinners would be a portrait of juxtaposition. My pack stood by as I hunched over my tiny gas burner, source of the flame that would carry me through this vast and magnificent world. Well, the flame that would cook the pasta that would carry me through. I got her going and stood back, watching the modest blue fire flicker and dance, so comically diminutive in the expanses she would avail to me.

The fjord waters fronting Igaliku lazed in dark, regal silence. Behind me, the slopes surrounding Narsarsuk rose up into the clouds. My pasta went down like champagne. Then for dessert I gulped down the cool air and pondered a logistical decision. Up above there was a valley splitting the mountains standing between me and the Black River. Or I could take on the river delta spreading out across the lowlands and tumbling into Erik's Fjord. Staring at my wet shoes it didn't take much to choose the higher, drier road. Along this valley route I'd most assuredly have fewer creeks and streams to wade through or throw discarded gates at. But there was the very real possibility of coming face to face with a wide, deep, and very cold river that, as far as I could tell from my maps, did not have a name. Or a bridge.

The lush green coastal belt, half-hidden in the morning fog, fell away as I began my climb toward the Great Valley (as I deemed it). My boots kicked up swirls of dust and sand; large boulders sat quietly at the feet of the great gray mountains. Danger signs appeared, in the form of patches of snow and dirty ice. The rushing river growled louder with each passing minute, like an animal that hasn't eaten anything – or anyone – in a while.

Moss and low grasses shivered among the stones lining the water's edge. The wildflowers I'd been seeing seemed to have been scared right off. I walked along, searching for a place to cross. But soon the encroaching mountain slopes forced me up against the banks and I had no choice left but to face fate and step into the gullet of the beast.

I changed shoes. I breathed in deep. Then with one foot in I thought of Vinska Gora and took off like a startled marmot.

Mind so consumed with visions of death and home, I have no recollection of feeling the cold rushing water as it tried to swallow me whole, legs first. When I opened my eyes there I was though, legs soaking wet, standing on a crest of dry land beneath my wobbly body.

Small victory for this still-warm-blooded creature; I had to take a moment to capture the occasion. I sat my tripod on a rock, firm and steady. The breezes drifted into nothing. But the timer on my camera was doing his own marmot impression and kept clicking before I could get settled into my relaxing in the grass pose. I felt kind of silly, all alone out there, but I had yet to be in any of my own pictures and I really wanted this shot. I might have been there fighting with my Nikon until dark set in if not for the view I suddenly noticed was waiting on the far side of the small hill rising up in front of me.

The land out there was desolate. Empty. Yet so full. The sky had cleared, blowing me away with an incredible view of the land before me and the glacier-laced mountains in the distance. Only the highest peak still wore a cloud cap – a crown for a king towering over his rocky minions. I went back and gathered up my camera; this was a fair bit more photo-worthy than a guy with wet feet lying in the grass.

Atop the hill the path flattened out, bringing me upon a pair of lakes so perfect they'd be surrounded by tourists in any other part of the world. The land was changing faces again, and I was making good headway. River-crossings and moody cameras;

was there nothing out here that could stop me? A stern answer soon came at me, in the unmistakable rumble of falling rocks.

I looked around. The land was still as a painting. But out there somewhere the land was moving. Greenland was alive. And, at least for the moment, so was I.

The lake area turned swampy. The only persisting signs of life were patches of moss and Niviarsiaq, the 'young girl,' Greenland's national flower. I trudged through the thickening slop; I came across no humans, saw no animals, spotted nary a footprint. The only sounds were my boots and my breathing. It was just me and the soggy land – and my monster rucksack trying to drive me right into the mud. Slogging through this squishy terrain made quick work of my energy and my spirits, so high just a short while ago. Greenland, I was fast learning, could be a real bitch. It was two hours since my marmot river skitter; I had been walking non-stop ever since. There was nowhere to set my pack down, save for the mud. But to hell with it, it was either me or him.

I was already shaking out my shoulders when he hit the ground like a huge wet slug. I stretched my back and rolled my neck in tired circles – and noticed the clouds were making a quick return. I scanned the horizon and wondered if the person who coined the phrase 'no rest for the weary' had ever been to Greenland.

I lurched on between the lakes, hopping from rock to rock, praying I'd reach the other side before sinking and becoming a permanent fixture in the sub-Arctic landscape. After a modest climb out of the swamp the land dipped off again; I descended very slowly, eyes fixed on the raging Qooqqup Kuua River.

A mix of resignation and fear rose up from my gut, flooding my mouth like used toothpaste. I studied the mud patterns on my boots as I toed the dropoff, water rushing angrily by two feet below. If all I had to look forward to was slop and wet socks, if not a wet and wild exit from life on this Earth, I might as well go back and hang out with Jörg. I scratched my head and looked around – and only then noticed the most incredible, most beautiful scene to ever fill my eyes. So far.

Tantalizing, tormenting, tempestuous Greenland...

Icebergs were calving off the Qoorqut Glacier at the end of the fjord in the distance. The rushing Qooqqup Kuua roared across the land and raced downhill, crashing with a hundred white fists into the Qooroq Ice Fjord, creating an undoubtedly impassable delta. The water was carrying with it enormous amounts of sand and silt, turning the dark green sea at the edge of the fjord a thick brownish-gray. The coast lay blanketed in lighter greens, spotted with violet flowers. And though I conceded this river would physically keep me from it all, there was nothing she could do to keep me from enjoying the view.

An hour later I was sitting on a level patch of terra firma in front of a small fire of sticks and twigs I'd scraped together. A thin column of smoke rose up, symbolizing to the world my continuing existence or something cheesy like that. As evening drew on I crawled into my tent. And with two days of walking now in my system I lay in my bag like I'd been nailed there, mind entirely subsumed by a wonderfully deep sleep.

Yet I woke up in the middle of the night, my curiosity

overriding my weary system. I peeked out the door and peered into the darkness. I couldn't see or hear a thing. The world sat in utter silence. The dark was enveloping. I was astonished. For this was almost the end of summer above the sixty-first parallel. Yet the clouds were thick enough to blot the midnight sun from the sky.

The next time I opened my eyes the world had taken on a soft, benevolent light. The weather forecast at the tourist office had said to expect the rains to hit by now. Other sources of information on the southern region held slightly different opinions as to what the day and the week would bring. Greenlanders themselves don't seem to pay much attention to weather forecasts; they just keep the worst possibilities in mind.

I pulled on my jacket and walked down to the river, rushing steadily by fifty meters below camp. Bent over, filling my bottle with water for breakfast, I heard for the second time the sound of falling rocks. Big ones, I surmised, as the rumbling was coming from the far side of Narsarsuk, the highest mountain around. Despite her tumultuous nature, Greenland seemed at least fair in reminding me from time to time that she could bury me in an instant.

The second full day of my trek – and the second day of my life I would be completely, utterly alone. As the ground led me down toward the banks of the Qooroq Ice Fjord the tundra turned to mush once again. But no matter; I had a master plan of attack. Resigned to missing out on a view of Lake Motzfeld, I would instead hike around the base of Narsarsuk – known to most outsiders as Mt. Burfjeld – and circle back to Igaliku (before the next rockslide if all went well).

I was excited. How could such a simple plan go awry?

The fjord was choked with ice shelves. I strolled along in full view of mountains and glaciers and a million scattered flowers. The vast beauty of Nature. God's last garden. The purity of the end of the world. Until I came upon four big dirty blue barrels. On the lids I could make out the names of those who used them to store food for trekking expeditions. I also noticed a kind of metal rod poking up from the middle of the four bins, similar to piping of some kind but more resembling...*a rifle?*

So much for God's unblemished garden.

After a moment of unease I decided to take a peek inside. This was of course out of mere curiosity; I had plenty of food, certainly none of it less tasty than anything left out here in a barrel for who knew how long. The first two bins were shut tight though – and as I reached across to check the others I found myself literally staring down the barrel of that rifle.

One of the first things I learned about camping in the wild (meaning anywhere outside) was that animals don't care whose food they are smelling. If they are hungry – and most animals walking around out there are – they will gladly help themselves to your hamburger meat. If they are big enough and hungry enough they will then help themselves to you.

Those barrels might have simply been shut tight against the elements. But the rifle, I was pretty sure, wasn't there to help fend off the weather. I looked around at the vast stillness. What was waiting for me out there?

I walked on, taking false comfort in the fact that I was the only animal in sight.

I listened to the voices rising from the water. I swore I could hear the delicate sound of the melting ice, dripping from the sharply angled bergs onto the surface of the freezing fjord. The rolling and turning plates of ice made louder, angrier noises as they scraped up against each other. The groan and crash of a calving iceberg rose up from somewhere out of sight. The high sloping mountains were mirrored in the water, now a turquoise blue, reflection deformed with the rolling, pitching floes. And for all the ice and icy waters, the sun was so warm I could walk comfortably in a t-shirt.

The calm, non-meat-eating scenery was soothing to my soul. For the moment I couldn't see anything resembling a path, but the mountains and the water guided me along – taking my mind off the significance of the massive rocks littering the land up ahead. The ground rose and fell, gentle slopes growing steeper as the mountains and the water closed in, kind of like a trash compactor now that I think about it. Boulders crowded against each other; I started climbing and squeezing through (boulders, apparently, are not worthy of denotation on some maps) until I looked up and spotted a break in the mountain ridge looming high overhead. This was the pass (I'd figured from my map that didn't point out passes either) that would lead me back into the Great Valley and on back to Igaliku. This was the passage that would open the peninsula up to me and propel me toward my goal.

If I could get to it.

I leaned against a boulder and stared. This so-called pass was sitting hundreds of meters above me, atop a towering rock wall buttressed by an equally formidable mountainside falling right off into the fjord. None of this was supposed to be here. This was supposed to be a hill, not a rampart. Hesitantly I unfolded my map. Had I miscalculated distance and slope and scale?

Like it made a difference now.

The land was clearly impassable. I was at a dead end. Or a dead beginning, as I was now further from my destination than I would be at any other point on the trek – assuming I'd learn anything from all of this.

I stared at the lines and markings on my map, the desolate voices of Greenland taunting me. There was something heavy in me – and something heavier hanging over me. Standing at the foot of the most recognizable mountain on the Qaqortoq Peninsula I felt a million miles from the rest of the world. I was alone in the vastness. The isolation roared in my head.

Rivers can become impassable torrents...

I glanced down at my t-shirt, tiny dots of sweat like omens.

For the first time on the trek – and in my life – I felt a real, measurable danger. Though only a couple days' walk from Igaliku, I could conceivably be stuck out here by myself for a very, very long time. And I only knew now what it truly meant to have to dig in and excise the doubts and dark thoughts that can form in one's mind. This wasn't a river crossing, where all I really needed were extra shoes and a bit of balance. This, suddenly, was an encounter with the possibility of the worst. Maybe this would turn out to be nothing. Maybe I'd be fine. But maybe, it suddenly seemed, was all I had.

Everything else was up to Greenland and her whims.

At least I didn't need a rifle...for the moment.

So I turned back and walked again among the magnificent scenery. I walked for the remainder of the day, circling back around the north side of brooding, ambivalent Narsarsuk, finally setting up camp virtually a stone's throw closer to Igaliku than the night before. An entire day – for a few hundred yards. It felt like the Blair Witch Project. As I let my pack drop to the ground I tried to find a speckle of consolation in an age-old bit of wisdom: tiny steps make up the longest journey. Though there's no allowance for the fatal implications of the sudden appearance of a torrential glacial river in there.

I found a patch of moss on high ground and lazed through the motions of camping. I fell asleep in a fog. I woke up in the same. The path back to civilization wore a hundred shades of gray. Only near the pass in the Great Valley did I catch a glimpse of blue sky. I could see through to one high mountain peak, painted a soft pinkish-red, glowing like a torch for me in the otherwise dim afternoon. More cheesy symbolism, sure, but at the time I needed all the boost I could come up with.

Years before, gazing at the photographs in a book titled 'The Unknown Mountains of Eastern Greenland,' I wished I could one day see those incredible colors for myself. Now here they were before me – soft, brilliant glimpses of the pastels of the North. And right there, in the middle of the mountains at the bottom of Greenland, in the kind of moment that eludes adequate words, I threw my rucksack to the ground. I closed my eyes; I lifted my head. I think I spread my arms. And I felt myself soaking in the transcendant beauty of the moment. This land was good. God's garden did exist. I was alone, but I was alive. And really, I knew I would indeed live to tell my modest tales.

As I bent down to pick up my pack I recognized in the soft sand the faint traces of footprints. Staring, mind still floating, I realized they were mine.

In the next moment the mountaintop was no longer visible. The only color I saw was in the small patch of flowers nearby. At first glance they seemed to be growing right out of the rocks, but looking closer I could see the earth underneath, nurturing enough at least for these modest, ambitious flowers.

The variegated flora found in the Arctic can be a special experience for the hiker. Arctic winters are characterized by extremely low temperatures and strong winds, but in the short summer the land explodes in a full-color palette of vegetation. There is quite a variety of plant life in the Arctic, actually. There are more than 250 varieties of flowers, and still more kinds of lichens and mosses. The arctic tundra is generally acidic and poor in nitrogen, and as the ground underneath is permanently frozen (for now), plants must pump all their nutrients up from the top few centimeters of earth. Most Arctic flora is perennial, a very important aspect of survival. In the span of the short arctic summer the plant life is faced with the critical task of blooming and producing seeds for the next generation.

My gentle thoughts of flowers were slowly sucked away as what had been lurking in the back of my mind came scratching back to the fore: I was going to have to cross that rollicking river again. My trepidation rose as the water growled louder – rivers don't ease up on you just because they've seen you before. But as I swapped my boots for my still-wet shoes I felt myself evolving, at least a little.

There was a bit less fright in my marmot dance this time.

The river widened, faster, more hectic as it advanced toward the mouth of the valley. The mountain walls began to curve away; the trail dipped down. And a loose cluster of houses appeared in the distance, seemingly close enough to reach out and touch though I was still three hours away. But just seeing the tiny village of Igaliku again was a beautiful, beautiful thing. The weather was good; my existence was intact. My spirits were once again on the rise.

When I came back to the site of my first river crossing I noticed my footprints had disappeared. The wooden gate that was my bridge was gone too. As I sat down to put my wet shoes on again I realized my initial trepidation in fording rivers had faded into almost nothing. I could scarcely remember the fears I'd felt at the outset; fears grounded in and fed by the unknowns – of this land and of the resources inside me. What this might mean if I were eventually faced with Greenland's worst, of course, remained to be seen.

Among the scattered houses of town I noticed three tents

pitched on a lush swath of grass. They didn't seem to be encroaching on anyone's space – if such a concept could even exist here – but still the trio of tents appeared a bit out of place. Nearby a couple of women were watching over a loose swarm of children. I smiled as I approached, preparing in my head some possible hand gestures for tent and camp and okay.

'Hello,' one of them said as I was about to launch into my pantomime. And I began laughing, I suppose at my ignorant disbelief that the first person I tried to talk to might speak even middling English. Without any idiotic gesticulation I asked her if it was all right to pitch my tent somewhere in the village.

Her face dropped in confusion. 'This is Greenland, isn't it?' And she got back to her kids, letting me decide for myself what she meant.

With a half wave I turned and headed for the youth hostel, a bright red longhouse of sorts. Inside a group of Danes told me not to worry about anything and just camp wherever. They also told me where I could take a shower. *Ah, a shower!* Fired up for a long-awaited date with hot soapy water I marched back outside, shrugged my pack off my shoulders and got to setting up my tent.

The group of children, oblivious to me a few minutes ago, was now a cluster of eyes, watching me in unsettling quiet. I smiled at them. They giggled and shied away, not knowing what else to do. The woman I'd spoken briefly with nodded, as if to confirm the fact that I knew she was right about something. I glanced over her entourage and winked. 'You camping too?' She giggled and explained how she was chaperoning this group of school children from Qaqortoq, of all places. Then she went on to tell me about her own travels around Europe. She was one of those very enthusiastic and genuine types, even asking me to join her for a cup of coffee in the village later. I must have been pretty ripe by this point, as she then took it upon herself to point out the shower room to me, along with the coin-op laundry, a room for drying wet clothes, and the hostel kitchen and dining area. *'The showers are communal,'* she went on to explain. *'In the height of winter this is the only place you'll find hot running water.'* But this being August I'd probably have the showers all to myself. I waved good-bye to the kids that hadn't completely lost interest and headed for a scrub-down.

The outer room was a small rectangle open to the elements, outfitted with a row of sinks. I ducked into the shower to strip my clothes off, only at that moment realizing just how horrid a stench I was giving off. Once down to my boxers it occurred to me I'd forgotten soap and shampoo, and I slipped out to dig them out of my pack. And right at that moment this guy walks into the room, steps right past me, goes into the showers and locks the door. In the next second the sound of hot water comes blasting out of the pipes. I stood there in my boxers and stared. And clenched my fists and cursed. And shivered.

With no better options immediately available, I took out my razor and got to shaving my face.

The fiend emerged and scampered off while I was still half-covered in lather. Once showered and changed myself, I walked outside to see my chaperone friend standing nearby, a telling look on her face. 'Interesting,' I said, no other words coming to me. She smiled apologeticially. *'This is Greenland, isn't it?'*

A notable site in Igalaku – 'Garðar' in Old Norse – are the ruins of the very first cathedral in the New World. Begun in 1126 with the arrival of Bishop Arnaldur, the first Bishop of Greenland, the cathedral was built in honor of St. Nikolai, the patron saint of seamen. I was chomping at the bit to see my first ruins, particularly some of such significance. The evening, however, was getting on; I'd have time for an initial gander but there was even now scant daylight for taking photographs. I'd be back tomorrow either way. So I put Bishop Arnaldur on hold and instead took a contemplative look around town.

In Greenland there seems a sort of circular rhythm to life. Stones that fall from old buildings like St. Nikolai are gathered up and used for other buildings, many of these over a hundred years old. Thus it is said some people in Greenland live in truly sacred homes. Around the houses throughout the village most of the grass was mowed; where it wasn't, buttercup were blossoming all over. I drank in the juxtaposition; Greenland's beauty adheres to no boundaries.

Perhaps unsurprisingly, the pace of life in settlements like Igaliku is very slow. Smaller villages usually have a single small grocery store, open a few hours a day and located in the center of town, which is normally right off the pier. A supply ship will come, twice a week or so, with food to replenish the shelves. Often sharing the same building with the grocery are a post office and a bank. For any sort of major purchase or simply a day of shopping, a trip to the nearest 'big' town is required. Transportation between towns is by ferry, family motorboat or, sometimes, helicopter.

As in many other settlements there is a Protestant church in Igaliku, the village priest lighting candles for Mass each Sunday. The children attend primary school here during the week, but when they reach junior high school they go off to boarding schools in the larger settlements. There is a small power station buzzing and rumbling away in the background at all times, supplying the town's inhabitants with electricity. In the evening the adults sit around and watch satellite TV, while the kids huddle together and play computer games. Some of the more sprawling villages even boast lines of streetlights.

Settlements differ greatly in size, from ten (or sometimes even less) to several hundred or a few thousand people. Farms are scattered, occupying vast swaths of land where ranchers breed sheep and hunt deer. For travelers accommodation can usually be found in hostels, or in cabins or school buildings. Information on these can be found in some of those 'bigger' towns. Igaliku, human population 50, was not one of them. But the locals are always happy to help out in any way they can. Except in the showers of course.

The sub-Arctic climate is much more favorable under the protection of the deep-cutting fjords, where you'll find most of Greenland's sheep farms. Hunting and, predictably, fishing are the prevailing forms of self-suffiency in the coastal settlements. This is traditional Greenland, where people still depend upon what nature will afford them. Danish immigrants living here are all too happy to tell you this. The path ahead of me is long still, on foot to Qaqortoq and then by ferry to Aappilattoq. There, in Greenland's southernmost communes, where hunting and fishing are the sole means of survival, would I experience the life of this island at its purest.

Under favorable morning skies I struck out for the ruins of St. Nikolai. By strike out I really mean walk across a field and up a short slope. Though the ruins don't exactly stand out, I still found them interesting, perhaps as one might consider Elvis Presley's grave intriguing. Though the few stones still standing reach no higher than a couple of meters, they had a special aura about them. These ruins, these one-ton blocks of cut stone, sit as testament to people who braved the harshest of elements in order to carve out a life for themselves – a life not far removed from mere survival – and yet still had it in them not simply to build a church, but to create with their hands something we in the modern age could perhaps not fathom to even be possible without our machines, in any climate.

I walked through the stone doorway. I breathed in the silent history, still palatable after a thousand frozen winters. The distance in kilometers I was from home seemed much greater than the time separating me from Bishop Arnaldur.

I stepped quietly, sensing an intangible connection to a time that no longer existed. And I wondered if maybe I had been here before – a long, long time ago.

I strolled one final loop through Igaliku, the thought seeping in that I had never experienced quite such a peaceful, quiet village. And I found myself wondering if there really was anything left to see on this vast island - besides hungry polar bears but I'd not stick around for that tour.

I took my deliberate sweet time climbing back up to the dirt and gravel of the Royal Way, soaking in the vibe of a place I'd probably never see again. Along the side of the road children played in small groups, pushing plastic tractors and bulldozers around. When they had enough they parked them in a line along the edge of the grass; only their quiet laughter broke the silence of the place. That and the occasional unregistered four-by-four passing by.

Midday was approaching when I set off up a path leading away from the village and toward my faraway destination of Qaqortoq. The trail rose sharply; comforting were the simple signposts pointing me in the right direction, leading me higher up over and through the incorrigible rocks of Greenland. Here and there I had to jump over a small stream. As I looked back the houses of Igaliku seemed so small against the land, spread out behind and below. The path rose once more, then dipped, and Igaliku was gone, nothing in front of me but the wide open expanses of the Qaqortoq Peninsula

The sparkling waters of Erik's Fjord lay several hundred meters below, off to the west. To my left the land rose gently before sweeping suddenly up into the mountains. Cottonweed swayed in the light breeze; I spotted a gentian flower here and there, painted blue and white and yellow. Low grass and scrub, creeping mosses and lichens; all growing on top of the stones hidden underneath.

The sound of rushing water drifted into my ears, growing louder and clearer with each passing minute. I determined it to be a waterfall, as there is no other sound quite like it. But I crested a gentle incline and saw that I was wrong – or at least not quite right. Tumbling down, splashing over the land were three sloping waterfalls, each falling into a pool deep enough for a dip. From each of these a shin-deep stream bounced and bubbled further downhill. On a warm summer day, I thought, this would be the perfect place to kick back and keep cool; get your friends together, pack some snacks and a few beers and have at nature. But then I remembered where I was.

Here in Greenland, on a warm enough day, or after a string of warm days, this playful waterpark would probably turn into a raging, sweeping river. The pools would disappear in a deluge of icemelt; those tumbling streams would become one rushing torrent, sweeping you and your friends and your beer down to the bottom of the fjord below.

I stepped easily across the shallow river, watching the water lick at my boots, wondering if things would be any different if Clemens were around.

On the far side of the fjord the shiny metal roof of an isolated farmhouse sat bright against the greens and grays of the Narsaq Peninsula. Further north, Erik the Red country was now also visible, captured between the deep blue-green fjord, populated with small icebergs, and the crystal clear arctic air.

The path I walked was gently worn, hinting at the hundred or so pairs of boots she sees in a year. The sound of the rushing waters faded, leaving me with nothing to listen to but my lazy breath. The sun was shining; small clouds were drifting in and out of heaven; an occasional breeze kicked up. I hadn't had lunch and I didn't care. Only a moment to enjoy the sight of a small lake broke my easy rhythm.

Staring at the clear, shallow water at my feet I saw that the lakebed seemed to barely slope away. Five, ten meters out, I could still see the bottom. If this were any indication, the bottom of the lake was shaped something like a dinner plate. I chucked a rock into the middle of the water – which told me only that it was at least as deep as a rock out there.

A walk around the dinner plate and up the creek spilling into it brought me to a larger one, possibly as deep as a contact lens as it was in turn fed by a third lake, larger still and barely higher than this second one now at my feet. Silver mountains, several miles in the distance yet still towering over me, reflected in the dark lake waters. The sun hung low in the sky, painting black the rounded rocky islets poking up through the surface of this largest lake (at least as deep as a pie plate), making them appear as a crocodile plying the water. I stepped through the shallow creek separating these two higher lakes and walked on, the air cooling as the sun continued rolling toward the horizon.

It was my ritual now to begin late in the afternoon to search for an agreeable place to camp. A feathery bed of moss was always welcome. Fresh water nearby was a must. Fortunately in God's garden these two are often found in fair proximity. Having found such a spot, I would feast on pasta and cocoa and stretch out on a mattress of green.

Seriously, how can anyone choose Waikiki over this?

I was feeling light, bouncing down the easy slope of the land toward the rough circle of dark green water a hundred meters below me. Another night, another lakefront home, and plenty of daylight remaining to enjoy it. I jumped over a meter-wide stream – and almost fell in. Not for nothing, mind you; then again, not for much. Right smack in the middle of the water was a big rock – a smooth, flat, boot-sized stepping stone, too perfectly placed for whimsical Greenland. The peculiarity was striking. The odds had to be astronomical.

Where but in Greenland does one think of such things?

Down by the edge of my lake I looked around for something to suggest someone had been here before. But I saw nothing. Not a footprint, nor a charred bit of firewood, not even a candy wrapper. That rock was the only piece of evidence, if it was even that, to indicate another human being had ever walked this land.

I pitched my tent before finally sitting down, taking in the view of the land for twenty perfectly silent minutes.

Relaxing next to my lake I felt like the King of Greenland, no crown on my head though I didn't need one. (Nor did I need a rifle to protect my land. Yet.) I was developing a good rhythm in my pace. The challenge of a full day's hike was morphing into routine. I felt a little less tired at the end of each successive day. And with this, my mind returned to the misty, mysterious world I first encountered way back in my living room: *Who was the last Viking on Greenland? What was it like to watch the horizon, waiting for a ship to rescue him from this place, to take him back to Iceland or maybe Norway?* My thoughts then turned to Clemens and his extrapolations on the regions and people of Greenland.

I recalled the pictures he showed me of Paradise Valley, filled with that mystical orange light I had yet to discover for myself. Memories of the stories Clemens told me, of trekking through the Kangerlussuaq region, brought images to mind of a huge valley dotted with grazing musk ox, too many to count. Another photo I saw was of an Inuit family, standing outside their seal skin tents. It was summertime, and well-apparent that life on the island hadn't changed much through the centuries. Only a few details testified to the modern European influence: their clothing, their fishing rods, their tomato ketchup. If I hadn't seen this photograph I would not have believed that there were people still lingering along the fringes of the Iron Age. Were they resisting the onslaught of progress? Was it slow in reaching this place at the end of the world? Did they just not know? These questions played in my head until a previous Clemens story crowded them out.

'Yes, you appear quite capable,' the folks at the Narsarsuaq tourist center conceded. But the recent warm spell was threatening to turn a glacial river into an insurmountable obstacle. Crossing over was presently possible; getting back might not be. Of course Clemens went off anyway – and ended

up wandering the land for four days before spotting that ship and shooting off his signal flare.

I smiled, picturing the scene. Such tales have always bred in me both excitement and fear that I too might someday end up nose to nose with uncertainty, vulnerability and Fate. Clemens had put his life on his shoulders and gone off in search of adventure, without cell phone or radio contact or any other such crutches for survival. He put himself at the mercy of Greenland's whims and survived.

I love listening to stories like this. They are rare and thus exceptional, as are the people who can tell them. From these one can find strength and energy in oneself. It is a great feeling when you come to realize such people are not born, but forged through trial and fire – or in this case a deluge of icy water.

Clemens had met me at the train station on a beautiful Viennese evening. We went by streetcar through town, past some of the most beautiful examples of art and architecture known to man, to spend some time sharing our love of the North and relishing those moments of solitude and pathless terrain where strategy, knowledge and courage with a capital C are all we have to rely upon. The big difference was, Clemens had already lived these moments. I had yet to step off into the wild on my own. Now here I was, my first brush with mortal uncertainty behind me. If I managed to avoid any torrential glacial rivers, perhaps my adventure would pass without any Clemens-esque near-death experiences. Though the stories would be good.

My growling stomach brought me back down to Earth, and I fired up another gourmet dinner. I'd made rice at the hostel knowing that out on my trek I'd be relegated to a steady diet of pasta, which takes much less time to cook and uses much less precious fuel. Plus having a bag of rice in your pack doesn't make running from polar bears any easier.

A technical engineer by education, I was keenly aware of the necessity of conserving fuel (as would be anyone with a GED in common sense I guess). At home in the Spring I'd conducted a few experiments, cooking and keeping careful track of how much gas I consumed with each meal. I didn't, however, factor in certain effects of the weather in Greenland. Only when I was out there did I realize how quickly my dinner could go cold once the gas was off. *A minor in meteorology would have been good* I thought, shoving my dinner down my throat.

In Greenland, when the sun sets and the air cools, large amounts of moisture get sucked off the surface of the sea. As per protocol, the fog came crawling in from the water as this evening wore on. I camp a fair bit above sea level whenever possible, to delay for a while longer the inevitable end of the day. Then before the fog totally engulfs the land I take a good look at my surroundings. If the morning turns into something like pea soup I want to at least have given myself a chance of heading off in the right direction. It's one simple but effective way of dealing with the pesky Far North.

For dealing with the frigid Arctic soil, I have a Thermarest exactly fifty-one centimeters wide – meaning I have less than two feet of room for not only my body but my sleeping bag as well, its twenty-below rating evidently invalid on ground above the sixtieth parallel. I roll over in my sleep, off my mat and onto the plastic tent floor, and the frozen tundra lurking underneath wakes me up faster than any alarm clock I've ever met. To Trek Sport's credit, if I do manage to keep myself on my mat I can sleep in boxers in that bag, even in sub-zero air temperatures. The ground's icy fingers, though, remain an unavoidable threat to a good night's rest.

I was up by seven-thirty, as had become my routine. I needed an hour to cook breakfast, wolf it down, break camp and pack up. I'd prepared enough rations for the trip to Qaqortoq plus two extra days' worth of muesli, powdered milk, powdered chocolate, instant coffee, tea and cocoa. Considering the circumstances, I was happy with the variety. I packed it all up with my rucksack balancing on a rock so I wouldn't have to lift her so far once her strings were cinched. Small things, I tell myself, add up in the long run. And today she was standing at attention, making the start of my day just a little bit easier.

The morning fog was thick but I was feeling good as I set off, following the same relatively worn path I'd by now come to recognize. Trails have a habit of fading on patches of detritus though, particularly in a fog that is thickening by the second. Before I knew it I was shuffling like a mole, squinting at the ground at my boots, searching for hints of the feet that had come before me – and knew where they were going. Like I said, I always make it a point to memorize the beginning of a day's trek; that is, until my spirits start running too high and I forget where I am and what it still takes to get out of there. Any preparatory efforts might have proven moot anyway. The fog was ridiculously dense, even here at this high altitude. Visibility was all of ten meters. I plodded forward, the ghost of Clemens leading me through the haze – a humorous thought replaced suddenly with the very unfunny figure of an animal creeping out of the mist before me.

I froze. *Great.* Misreading maps and running out of fuel can make for dire circumstances – but there's not a lot of time to ponder and regroup when you're alone in the wild staring down a baby polar bear...*with long ears?* I bent down, creeping forward under the weight of my pack, trying for a better look at this timid little rabbit.

My heart slowed back down as I stepped off the faintly visible trail leading to Hvalsey. I moved toward Fluffy; he hopped a few feet away. I waited and eased ahead again; my counterpart kept his languid distance. We moved like this, creeping and hopping, until a loose rock under my boot sent my friend bouncing out of sight. And suddenly there I was, in a relentless fog, the trail suddenly gone. I tried to retrace my steps, but the path had magically evaporated. No problem, I assured myself. The mountain ridge I'm heading for is right in front of me.

Somewhere.

Thirty minutes walking uphill brought me to a pass; down below in the clearing air I spotted a lake, gray as the low-lying clouds. I remembered I had to pass by a lake, maybe two, to continue on toward Qaqortoq from this ridge. I had lost the trail for the moment, but this had to be the right place. How can a half-hour walk lead you to the wrong mountain?

I bounced downhill, the weather here on the other side of the peninsula much more favorable and generous. By the time the ground leveled out I was feeling good enough again to pause and treat myself to some good hot soup. A light wind picked up as well, giving me a chance to dry out my tent. Hauling a wet tent around on your back is mildly unpleasant; pitching and climbing into a wet tent pretty much sucks. Even in paradise.

After a longer break than I intended (I blame the view) I packed up again and rolled on down to the lake. And I walked along the left shore. And walked and walked. Forever, it began to seem. *Something's wrong*, I heard a voice telling me. It sounded like Clemens. I unfolded my map and stared. I was in a valley, as I should have been. But...was I in the wrong one? How many valleys were there around here? The lake next to me was at least a kilometer long; the one I was supposed to be walking alongside was no more than 300 meters. *A double minor in meteorology and cartography would have been good...*

I was faced with two choices, which in some circumstances can be more troublesome than one. I could backtrack and try to get back on my planned route (certainly not guaranteed), or forge ahead and figure it out and hope my emergency flares work. Either path I chose, as long as it eventually led southwest, would for all intents and purposes keep me moving forward. So I kept my boots pointed ahead of me and continued along the valley, expecting to eventually stumble upon the path I'd lost. The long lake eventually fell away behind me, soon replaced by another, then a third, dried up now but perhaps a real lake when my map was printed, seven years previous.

Along a hillside trail I came upon a herd of Icelandic horses. Shuffling their hooves at the sight of me and my pack, they seemed to present a shyness not seen in their siblings back in Iceland or their cousins from the rest of Scandinavia. Logical perhaps, for animals in a land with so few people. I stepped slowly toward them. I pulled open the zippered pocket keeping my camera warm and dry. With all the clouds and fog and long annoying lakes I'd had little opportunity to shoot any decent photos. And since I had no remotely useful trail to lose for the moment, I decided to try to get as close as possible for a shot of these beautiful creatures. Two, three soft steps toward them, then a hard scraping under my boot. I looked down – and noticed a straight line of stones at my feet.

Certainly odd. Quite unnatural. The remains, old if not ancient, of human activity. I walked a gentle circuit around them and discovered another set of stones, arranged in a neat oval. I let go of my camera and pulled out my map...and saw no markings anywhere on this part of the peninsula denoting these ruins I was now standing on. I scratched my head. Had I stumbled upon a missing piece of Greenlandic history? Losing my way, stalking polar hares and maneuvering for photographs of shy horses; was it all mere coincidence that I ended up standing on top of this gold mine of potential?

The ghosts of the land indeed.

Later I would pick up a detailed map of known Viking ruins and find this spot yet again unmarked. My dreams of finding new ruins materializing before me, I would spend the next few years contacting various museums in Greenland and Denmark, e-mailing them accounts of the two modest formations I'd found, plus a third I hadn't even noticed until I took a good look at the photos I'd taken. I asked them if they knew whether these sites had in fact ever been discovered, and if not, what might be the proper course of action. *Can I name them? Do I get my own show on cable?* But no one showed any interest in my discovery outside of the people at the museum in Qaqortoq. And even they seemed too disinterested to actually go look at them.

But for one moment, all alone among the mountains and the valleys of Qaqortoq, I had made my great discovery. And I mused about the strange twists one's path can take.

I spent several hours navigating that valley, on the wrong side of a mountain that for a while could have been anywhere or nowhere the fog was so thick. The lakes I weren't expecting to be there finally fell away, only to be replaced by a fjord that was supposed to be on the other side of me. Really, this should have had me reaching for my stash of signal rockets (a much less fear-inducing term than emergency flares). Yet I walked on, head high, taking in the beauty of my accidental side trip around Qaqortoq. And as the sun began to dip toward the horizon I found myself tripping back onto my original trail.

With the water on my left and the land rising sharply up to my right – the reverse of earlier in the day – I was, interestingly enough, back on my planned westward track. And for all I'd been through, I reached the ruins of the farmstead of Hvalsey with the sun still hovering well above the line of the distant sea.

The site is entirely surrounded by a five foot fence. This is more to keep any livestock out than keep the odd trekker away. There was, I believed, a ladder over the fence somewhere. Finding it was proving oddly difficult. Finally I clambered over the fence, my rucksack still on my back as I hadn't seen any fresh water around, in any form.

I took a cursory look around the ruins, but the growing, graying shadows shuttered out any possibility of capturing even one good photo. I turned away, hopeful for a sunny tomorrow – and found myself staring over at the ladder. A few minutes later I stumbled upon a gurgling stream that I swear didn't exist either before my fence climb.

Morning broke in a symphony composed of heaven. The air was so clear you'd think this place had never seen fog; the land lay clothed in blessed greens. A few lazy cirrostratus clouds contrasted with the cold blue arctic sky. In my entire trek, if I could have one day like this, it would be right here in Hvalsey.

By nine o'clock I was climbing over that ladder again, sun shining down on the mysteries that had been lurking in the foggy recesses of my mind for so long. Straight off I made a beeline for Hvalsey Church; as I approached her proud remains my steps slowed, a film I had seen as a boy, fifteen years in the past – *half my life ago* – replaying itself in my mind.

I stood back in reverence, next to the remains of a large building where perhaps traders had taken up accommodation. Flickering images of the Vikings, mysteriously disappearing from Greenland, flashed once more through my head. In the caverns of my imagination, questions whispered and echoed: *What happened to these Vikings? Why did they leave?* I stepped easily amidst the remnants of a town and a time gone by, picturing myself living among the people who made this place their home and their life.

I walked through the doors of Hvalsey Church; the hairs on my arms bristled. In that film this church was presented in a shroud of cloudy mystery; now here I stood, soaking up the clarity and glory of this mystical site. I thought of another film, a documentary on trekking in the south of Greenland, also shot in a thick fog so as to heighten the drama of the Vikings' extinction. But watching those cloudy images, my own wishes, my own dreams, were crystal clear. I had to go. I had to see. To stand there. And feel. Now, after fifteen years of dreaming here I was, alone at the end of the world, standing in the rubble of the biggest mystery of the Middle Ages.

What happened to the Vikings of Greenland?

It is written in the Icelandic chronicles that in 1409 a wedding ceremony was held in Hvalsey, in a parish church believed to have been built around 1300. Hvalsey was at the time the most important Scandinavian colony in all of Greenland. Two priests were present at the ceremony; the wedding vows were said to have been read through three times. Numerous Vikings who had settled in the area were also in attendance, along with a handful of crew members of an Icelandic merchant ship. Soon after the wedding, these crew members returned to Iceland.

This is the last record of the Vikings who occupied Greenland.

It is possible that as many as 500 people lived in Hvalsey during the early 1400's, but by the early part of the next century they had all disappeared. Around 1540 a German ship was blown off course, through the floating ice to the fields where the proud Viking colonies had been replaced by abandoned farms, silence and tranquility. After 500 years of Viking settlement, Greenland had once again been left to the cold, the ice, the sea and the Inuit.

But what happened? Why did these colonies, on the edge of the North Atlantic, disappear right when the discovery and exploration of the New World was picking up momentum?

The discovery and colonization of Greenland was a result of the migration of Scandinavians that began at the end of the 8th Century and continued on through to the middle of the 11th. Taking part in these Viking grabs, referred to by some as 'plundering expeditions,' were an array of Norwegians, Danes and Swedes. In the 8th Century the Vikings were thought to have the most advanced shipbuilding technology anywhere in the world, producing two major types of ships: drakkars and knorrs. Drakkars were quick warships, suited for lightning-fast attacks, while knorrs carried freight and merchant crews. These vessels were large, slow and quite difficult to navigate. Plying these knorrs through the torrid Atlantic, sailors were endlessly blown off course. These merchant seamen became something of accidental Vikings in this regard, beginning to move almost at random rather than sailing with a specific destination in mind. They first discovered the Faroe Islands in the early 800's, then Iceland in 860, Greenland around 980 and finally North America around the turn of the millenium.

The first records of the discovery of Greenland, though, date back to the beginning of the 10th Century. In approximately 920 a crew led by a man named Gunnbjörn Ulfsson was blown in a strong storm westward from Iceland, allowing them to catch sight of an unknown land in the distance. However, they returned to Iceland before exploring any further.

In 982 Erik the Red set sail west of Iceland in search of this rumored land. After only a few days at sea the crew reached the eastern coast of Greenland. Looking upon the land, Erik saw a region quite inhospitable, driving him southward. He completely bypassed Cape Farewell and turned north, navigating the western coast where he found innumerable fjords reaching deep into the land, protected by mountains and rich with grassy pastures, perfect for the grazing and breeding of stout, healthy cattle. The waters of the region were replete with fish; herds of wild caribou roamed the lush hills. After a full three years of exploration he returned to Iceland to recruit people to settle this new 'green land' with him. While perhaps understating the true extent of the icy side to this new and unknown territory, the green land that did exist was no less suitable for raising cattle than the fields of Iceland, where there was an ever-increasing shortage of farmable land. Thus it did not take long for him to find numerous inquisitive, adventurous souls to take him up on his invitation, and in 985 he led a fleet of ships from Iceland to Greenland

The majority settled near present-day Qaqortoq, which came to be known as the Eastern settlement. The rest navigated their way three hundred kilometers further north to establish their own oasis of green, named (aptly or oddly) the Western settlement.

Greenland from the first settlers to the mid-14th Century

Immigrants to this new territory replicated the farms in Iceland they left behind. Erik the Red settled with his family at the foot of a mountain on a long fjord, naming his claimed fields 'Brattahlid,' where the ruins of his farm are still visible today. Both the Eastern and Western settlements soon began to prosper, and as years turned into decades the people came pouring in. The Eastern settlement became the larger of the two, with approximately four thousand people living on close to two hundred farms. In the west, well over a thousand people occupied farms numbering around one hundred. The majority of these farms were scattered across the interior of the fjords, where the climate was more temperate.

Though still living in relatively small communities on a vast, largely unknown island of ice, these Scandinavian settlers were not by any means laboring in isolation. They enjoyed an abundance of resources sought by their fellow Europeans, who in turn were able to provide these new 'Greenlanders' with things they could not produce for themselves. The settlers traded caribou furs, seal skins, seal oil and wool with the Icelanders and Norwegians, who brought grain, iron, honey, corn and dyes. The northernmost settlements were also an important source of walrus meat and polar bear fur, both of which were in high demand in medieval

Europe. These Greenlanders were not confined to their own island either, finding their way to the Labrador region of Canada for the rich timber stores there. Testifying to this are relics and remains found on settlers' farms made from larch not known in Europe. Viking explorers are also known to have visited the east coast of North America by way of evidence of Viking ruins in Newfoundland, discovered in 1961.

All available findings point to the notion that these Viking settlements in Greenland flourished. Trade with the Norwegians had become an institution. Settlers built churches in both the east and west settlements – indeed a fair achievement for a people flirting daily with the very limits of survival. Ultimately though, the life of the Vikings in Greenland was covered by a thick veil of secrets. Limited evidence suggests they had left the Western settlement by the middle of the 14th Century. The last recorded event in the chronology of the Vikings of Greenland was the wedding in Hvalsey. After this, they simply disappeared over the horizon of history.

Danish archaeologists began excavating Viking settlements in Greenland after the first World War. Although they couldn't dig up any direct evidence about the mysterious disappearance of the Vikings, they developed a theory, at the time generally accepted, that explained things something like this:

In 1261 the Vikings in Greenland accepted rule by the Norwegian king, agreeing in turn to 'contribute' monetarily to the Kingdom. By virtue of this agreement, Norway succeeded in creating a trade monopoly with the Vikings of Greenland, prohibiting any and all transactions with foreign merchant ships. In exchange, the king promised to send at least one ship to Greenland each year to deliver commercial goods. But the settlers were collectively too poor to be paying the taxes levied by the king. Nor were they capable of producing enough goods to compete and trade equally. In time the church took over a full third of the inhabited fertile land, the local bishops demanding additional taxes from the already-struggling farmers. The majority of the people soon found themselves unwilling subjects of both the king and the church.

In the 14th Century a mini ice age overran the northern hemisphere. Farmers produced less and less hay as the short summers turned shorter and colder with each passing year. Thus they had less to feed their livestock during the increasingly long winters. So paltry were their trade offerings, and so increasingly demanding and dangerous the navigation of the growing obstacles of floating ice along the shore, fewer and fewer ships continued to bother maintaining commercial ties with Greenland. The king and the church virtually forgot about the settlers and their aggravated economic circumstances, and the inhabitants of Greenland watched helplessly as they became more and more isolated from Norway. The colder climate was also forcing the Inuit southward, where they began competing with the Vikings for the caribou, walrus, seals and polar bears. Some contend it is conceivable the Inuit turned to raiding the settlers' farms. Church representative Ivar Bardarson, who was living in the Eastern settlement during these unsettling times, reported to have traveled to the Western settlement in the mid-14th Century to find it abandoned, reasoning that the inhabitants had all left, died of hunger, or perhaps been killed by the Inuit.

In 1404 an Icelandic ship was blown off course, forcing the crew to spend several winters in Greenland. These crew members were the witnesses to the now-famous marriage in Hvalsey. And theirs was the last Viking ship to ever cast off from Greenland. For a century the remaining settlers battled and struggled for their survival. By the beginning of the 16th Century, the Vikings of Greenland had become an atrophied, mutilated race. Thus sounds the story told by their skeletons.

But is all this true?

This line of deduction rings insubstantial in explaining the Vikings' mysterious disappearance. One question that can be raised is: Did taxes and forced contributions really bring financial decimation to the colonies of Greenland? A thesis on the Greenlanders' acceptance of the Norwegian king as the colonies' ruler relies on ambiguous documentation written a century after the fact. It is generally accepted that the king demanded control over Greenland, but the question remains whether the inhabitants of Greenland, living on the edge of existence, accepted in practice the king's rule. It seems likely the Greenlandic Vikings struck commercial agreements with the king, but their dealings with the merchants points more toward a feudal loyalty. It is more probable that the Norwegian merchants, collecting taxes in the name of the king, were actually bringing goods obtained in Greenland directly back to their home regions rather to the king in Bergen.

It is also difficult to firmly conclude that the church gentry contributed to the economical demise of the Vikings of Greenland. In Iceland priests were as poor as church mice, dependent on the generosity and pity of their parishioners. Circumstances were probably quite similar in Greenland, where many of the wealthier farmers built their own churches. Thus the church most likely was not in a position to turn the farmers into their subjects, particularly on their own land. Thus as in Iceland, where people weren't paying church taxes, the settlers of Greenland most likey weren't in any practical sense subjects of the king or church, resembling the unbending independent attitude among the other transplanted Vikings scattered over the shores of the North Atlantic.

Impact of the Little Ice Age

The long cold period that enveloped the northern hemisphere from the beginning of the 14th Century certainly caused hardships for the inhabitants of Greenland. Navigation from Iceland and Norway through the denser, thicker pack ice now barricading the coast had indeed became a much more harrowing proposition. Coupled with the farmers' inability to produce adequate hay for their sheep and cattle during the long winters, traders saw little sense in maintaining their ties with the settlers. On their own in an increasingly hostile environment, farmers had to either start turning miracles in the use of their land or change their survival tactics. Remnants of waste heaps left among their ruins suggest that during these harsh times they moved toward a more seafood-based diet, subsisting mainly on fish and seal meat. Fishing nets have even been found in some settlement excavations, so perhaps we can assume with fair certainty the settlers were quick studies in the ways of fishing, providing them with an alternative to the depleted trade industry. Further interesting evidence – or lack of evidence – to their ultimate disappearance lies in their skeletal remains, which do not show any perceptible aggravations in their state of health, even with the plagues that were beginning to spread through Europe at the time. Thus it seems quite incorrect to claim the settlers would so quickly and completely have succumbed to this little ice age. Which may then lead to a rather interesting question:

Did Ivar Bardarson actually visit the Western settlement?

It is written in the chronicles that in 1350 Ivar Bardarson saw only wild horses, goats and cattle, with no signs of either Christians or pagans in the Western settlement. The Eastern settlement was described in great detail and mentioned often, while the west was hardly given a whisper. That the largest farm in the west region, Sandnes, was mentioned at all could simply have been a product of hearsay and not a conveyance of actual experience. It can hardly be argued that inhabitants were in fact leaving the Western settlement. Conditions were certainly becoming tougher, the cold summers driving many south toward the Eastern settlement. The population was decreasing, and men able to catch seals and fish were lacking in numbers. But some evidence suggests a number of the farms remained inhabited until the late 14th Century, the last of the settlers finally dying of old age. This is not evidence of a lost struggle with the cold, but a combination of some people deciding to leave the area and the rest staying behind to live out their lives.

Ivar Bardarson was sent from Norway to Greenland's Eastern settlement to act as the local church representative, supervising the instruction and ordination of new priests. He most likely also acted for the king in a sort of financial capacity. Though speculation rather than documentation, he could have claimed to have gone to the Western settlement in 1350 to bring to the settlers there a portion of the goods he'd transported to Greenland from Norway; then, stating the land was deserted, kept the goods under his control. He might have reasonably believed the settlement was in fact emptying out, as fewer and fewer people were moving to the Eastern settlement. Either way, Bardarson's widely-accepted claim that the Western settlement was completely abandoned by 1350 might help substantate the little ice age theory, but as there is evidence to point to the settlers' ability to survive the cold, albeit in smaller numbers, perhaps less credence should be placed in Bardarson's famous findings.

Did the Inuit attack the Vikings?

There was certainly some tension and conflict when the Vikings showed up on the land of the Inuit, but the Inuit in all likelihood didn't fall into fighting with the outsiders. Conflict was apparently a foreign concept to them. They lived mostly along the seaside, hunting seals and whales. The Vikings settled deeper in the fjords where the pastures were best. Thus the two probably didn't live in close enough proximity to each other to create tension that would lead to outright conflict. A harmonious co-existence would have been more beneficial to both sides, as the Inuit preferred the Vikings' iron tools while the Vikings were happy to trade for all the walrus skins, meat and ivory they could get.

Scandinavian objects and images of Vikings have even been discovered in Inuit homes. Their two cultures seemed to mix more than clash.

Did the settlers die out from isolation?

According to the official version of things, the Vikings disappeared from Greenland because of their isolation – Europe had given up on them by the mid-14th Century. But this theory doesn't hold adequate water as the settlers went on inhabiting their green land until around 1480. Archaeological evidence confirms that there even remained through this period some commercial bonds between Europe and the Viking settlers still living on the island.

While the western settlers had all vacated or died by the end of the 14th Century, those in the east continued to trade with English merchants. Among the ruins of a house in the Eastern settlement a black cross was discovered – an important artifact, as it had been made in Yorkshire, England. Found in another ruin was a knife from the 15th Century bearing a pattern characteristic of London at the time. Also dug up were pieces of kitchenware, painted with typical medieval European motifs, as well as clothes in graves, tailored in a style quite fashionable in Europe between 1440 and 1480. Further evidence of their existence continuing until the late 15th Century were three buildings erected on three of the largest of the area's farms. Similar structures have been found on Norway and Iceland, evidently constructed for important local public events. These three buildings in Greenland, used for communal activities and, perhaps, for housing the occasional visitor, were probably completed after 1420, though according to the above-mentioned official version of things the settlers had already begun their steady demise in the face of hunger and Inuit attacks.

Records of the Eastern settlement from the beginning of the 15th Century to 1540.

Who was the last visitor to Greenland? Who was the last Viking? The last visitors were most likely English merchants from Bristol, and perhaps a few other ports. Records show that in the 15th Century Englishmen were importing Atlantic cod from Iceland – and most likely from Greenland as well. Their first contacts were conceivably accidental, occurring as a crew of English seamen were pitched off course in the typically unforgiving Arctic waters and ended up beached in the vicinity of the Eastern settlement. As contact was established the Vikings in Greenland might have been rather encouraged by the prospect of producing cod and trading for things they did not have. Archaeological finds point to their contact with English ships lasting for most of the 15th Century. Atlantic cod was a much sought-after commodity in medieval Europe, as it was customary in the church on

Fridays and certain holidays to only eat fish. Cod oil was widely-used in Europe as well, as were objects made of wool. Demand for fur and ivory added to the settlers' fortunes, spurring them to hunt in the west for seal and walrus and contributing to the survival of the Eastern settlement for the whole of the 15th Century. Certain evidence hints at two merchant fleet owners from Bristol who may have even acted as the main traders with the Greenland Vikings, though it is certainly likely merchants from other ports were also in on the cod trade. A few Norwegian ships as well are said to have appeared along the southern Greenland coast in the 15th Century, each crew claiming to have been blown off course on their way to Iceland, perhaps in order to avoid having to pay taxes upon their return to Norway.

Excavations show that contact with the English lasted until approximately 1480. Archaeologists have yet to dig up anything from after this period. Why the merchants from Bristol would have ceased trade with the Vikings is not fully understood. Ships from Bristol have been discovered along the shores of Newfoundland, probably from the time before Christopher Columbus. They may have discovered the 'Grand Banks' of Newfoundland, best known for the rich Atlantic cod harvests. This may have led to the break with the Vikings of Greenland. This link to a brand new world was most likely the main culprit in ending the Eastern settlement on Greenland. It is not difficult to imagine the people feeling isolated from the world once the English gave up on them. Life had been hard enough. Now, alone, survival had become an even tougher task. Thus the people began thinking of a new, better life.

The population had decreased significantly even before 1480, when there were only about a hundred inhabitants. As in the west, the people of the Eastern settlement quietly, steadily left their fields and their land. Excavation of farms suggests the people loaded up all their personal belongings when they vacated, as very little evidence of their material existence was left behind. Icelandic records from this period are scarce, though most likely the Vikings of Greenland headed off for Iceland.

The first to leave were the younger and stronger folk, as well as those who owned ships. The older inhabitants and the shipless were driven by circumstance to stay behind. The crew of the German ship diverted from their route to Iceland in 1540, straight to the fields of the Eastern settlement, wrote down the details of what they saw: abandoned farms and silence, and the body of a man in a shed built for drying fish, still dressed in his woolen jacket and trousers made of seal skin. For the Vikings who remained, help had come too late. This man had perhaps gone through his last years as the last Viking of the Eastern settlement, left behind, alone on Greenland, to look to the horizon each day for the ship that would never come.

My imagination was still running wild as I bid Hvalsey farewell. Fanciful images of the first and last Vikings of Greenland, from Erik the Red to that man in the shed and all those in between, swirled in one great, hazy daydream in my mind.

Two hundred yards up the trail they were wiped away by the very real picture of a waist-deep forest of thick foliage in my way.

At least the size of a football field, this tangled mess of arctic bushes (to use the proper term) looked all but impassable. Trudging through a meter of snow with my six-year-old niece on my back would be about the equivalent. I scanned the steep rocky slopes crowding the leafy beast on both sides. *There has to be an easier way.* I pictured myself as Steve McQueen in The Great Escape, minus his army of shovels.

But plus one sheep?

From out of nowhere she came stumbling along, nosing her way along the fringes of the forest. *Maybe she knows a way through...* Sheep might not be at the apex of animal intelligence, but this bumbling little creature, surviving out here without Gore-Tex and cocoa powder, just might know her way around. With a stick in my hand and vague recollections of grade school and Sister Constansi in my head I started whacking at the grass, hoping my little wooly friend would lead me to her secret passageway. She paused and looked at me, took two steps, sniffed the bushes, looked at me, sniffed her rear, looked at me, sniffed and licked a couple leaves...

This was one lamb that would never see Qaqortoq.

cked the ground at her hooves and she sprang into the the enchanted forest, completely – and I really mean *completely* – disappearing on me. Immediately, and without a lot of deliberate thought, I began making up new and (for the moment) more fitting words to *Mary Had A Little Lamb*.

I stepped forward and leaned into the sticks and branches, singing to myself. (*Damjan caught a little lamb, brittle lamb, rock head bam...*) My sheep friend was neck-deep in the brush, fifteen yards away. She stopped and looked back, listening or laughing at me I'm still not sure. Either way, I wanted lamb chops for dinner, I didn't care how much fuel I'd have to use up. Frustration leading the way I bush-whacked my way straight through to the other side, by which time my dinner date had completely disappeared again.

A quick look around brought me to a rough path leading uphill. The faint feeling of a thousand burrs still scratching at my legs, I put my head down and plowed ahead until I reached a plateau beneath the summit of another nameless mountain. *Now,* I told myself, half out of breath. *Time for a break.* And for the next half hour I laid in the grass, swatting the occasional fly off my face.

The bloody nursery rhymes faded; the emotional burdens of my trek fell off my shoulders once again. I could feel the brakes of uncertainty within me easing. I had enough fuel for the time being; all my clothes were dry. Considering my remarkable sense of misdirection I could have fallen much further off track. A calm satisfaction seeped into me. A yellow glow crept over the green land as I resumed walking the hillsides, following my nascent confidence across a land without trails. Rivers no longer intimidated me. Thick swaths of brush were no match for me either now, sheep or no sheep. I walked the straightest, most direct way I could, as if that would help me regain whatever minutes and momentum I had lost. I was on my way. Moving forward. A trekker, once more invincible, conquering new territory with every sure stride.

I even entertained ideas that the feeling would last.

My first thought was of a Jules Verne novel as the crevice came into view. It might have been a simple discoloration in the earth; such was my tenuous hope as I closed in on this, the newest most difficult step of my journey. A fissure in the land, two yards across and a good fifteen feet deep, stretched across my path and on into forever on both sides. I searched for something to save me – like a huge wooden gate. But all I saw were grass and rocks and one heck of a hole in my way, long as the Grand Canyon as far as I could tell. The invincible trekker was once again a tiny dot in the vastness. This is what I get for choosing confidence as my guide instead of an updated map.

As I stared into the abyss the thought came rushing at me: I was going to have to jump it.

I scanned the horizon.

God, this place is desolate...

I stood on my toes; no other bottomless pits behind this one, to gobble up my crash-landing body if I made it that far.

I squared my feet and bent my knees, as if any amount of calisthenics would help me now. I shook off my rucksack and swung it around, ready to chuck it across. But then it occurred

77

to me: if my pack made it across and I didn't, my emergency flares, not to mention food and protection for a few days stuck in a hole in the ground, would be much more useful if I could get to them. And if I managed to drop my pack down this entrance to hell I had absolutely no way of retrieving it. *Should have done track and field* I told myself. But who ever took up the hammer throw or the long jump or pole vaulting in case they happened to meet a gaping huge crack in the ground?

After a few more moments of visualizing and contemplating I tightened my pack straps. I took a dozen steps backwards. I breathed in and out and sucked down a mouthful of water (this making me feel like a true long jumper). Then I took one more step back, sucked in two more breaths and started running.

My boots fell heavy on the ground, jarring my insides and my eyesight. The world in front of me bounced in a blur. The beast drew closer, yawning, waiting. Growling for all I knew. Five more steps...three...two?

Oh sh-!

And in a flash I was all arms and legs, flailing and skidding and fighting my pack as he kept pushing me forward, further over the lip of the monster. My body teetered. I gasped, or maybe cursed. The black hole showed me his throat.

I waited and waited, a full minute at least, hands on my knees, peering down into the center of the Earth.

The vacant soul of the underworld stared back at me. And I hate being stared at.

I walked back and took perhaps the last gulp of water of my life. And I took off running once more. And this time I jumped.

I soared. I plummeted. My rucksack propelled me forward through the air and then drove me into the ground. I could feel every one of my bones as my body hit the hard ground. My legs and arms and back crumpled, bending in ways and places I never knew they could. If anyone had seen me, they'd think I was finished for sure. Lying motionless among the lichens, I didn't know either. I wiggled my fingers and toes; I lifted my arms; and slowly, I got to my feet. I looked behind me, and up and down the length of the crevice – and somehow only now saw that I had chosen the worst, widest possible place to jump. Here and there and almost everywhere I saw much narrower expanses of nihilism and doom. I checked all my joints. None of them, thankfully, were able to do new things. Then I brushed off and adjusted my straps and continued on toward Qaqortoq, reacquainted with the idea that I would encounter endless obstacles along my way. But one challenge after another, I believed – because I had to – that I would always be able to meet them head on.

So with my confidence rising again, another dance with death behind me, the trek and the fear of the unknown was morphing into life's affirmation once more. A moment of triumph. A brave conqueror. Slayer of dragons and big ditches. A lone warrior in the cold wilderness – who couldn't believe how fast the ground in Greenland could freeze his tail.

Attempting another picture exaggerating my composure, begging my camera to hurry up and go click, I couldn't ignore the permafrost clawing my rear with her icy fingers.

I'd planned for this. And I was now just remembering *'Hey, I planned for this'* and pulled out a swatch of foamy rubbery stuff we in Slovenia call armaflex (named for a similar product used for insulating refrigeration and heating systems). This little yellow mat, you can say, saved my ass on more than just this occasion. Without it I would have to unroll and even blow up my thermarest whenever I wanted to rest my muscles without freezing my bones (or sitting on my pack, a simple idea that had somehow eluded me). And Qaqortoq would be that much further away.

I snapped my photo and walked on, the world around me, at least for the moment, shimmering in the sun.

Greenland, apart from the ubiquitous rocks and the occasional bottomless pit, is a world of soft light and pastel colors, a veritable goldmine of inspiration for artists of all kinds. It should come as no surprise then that a fair number and variety of artists came over from mainland Europe to settle here: photographers, painters, poets, writers. The verdant landscape, the deep ocean, the infinite blue dome – everything was such that it looked itself like it was just freshly painted. Perhaps Erik the Red himself was just as taken by the pastel greens in his eyes.

Walking through this supreme work of art I treated myself to mouthfuls of dried fruit, mainly pineapple and banana. I'd dehydrated them at home myself, adding a little sugar, giving the fruit a kind of caramelized coating. I also had with me a mega-sized box of chocolate cookies, so I was anything but under-sugared. I'd see later that I could have made my trek twice with all the snack food I was carrying.

Not that I'm complaining about having too many cookies.

Late in the afternoon the clouds rolled in (why not?) and I hiked the day's last few kilometers through a thickening fog. I braced myself against the strengthening wind as it whistled through my ears. It was a familiar sound now, a meandering, brusk melody I knew by heart. I passed a shepherd's hut, half crumbled to splinters. I spotted a beer crate, on one side the logo of a Danish brewery. *Don't need a fridge in this kitchen...* I came upon a fenced enclosure, too small for grazing, so most likely a place for keeping hay as it was gathered for the long winter. I checked markers and elevations on my map, noting paths and measuring my progress. I built a low circle of stone to keep the wind from fanning the flames from my stove and burning up my fuel. I shook the canister before hooking it up; still enough in there, it felt like, to last me to Qaqortoq. This as much as anything would help me get some decent sleep.

Liquid fuel is better than gas for one very practical reason. With gas it is all but impossible to tell how much fuel you have left. And knowing that you do have fuel left is, in a word, good. Having fire lends an emotioonal boost as well, especially on a trek like this. Flame is a companion in endless solitude. Fire is moral support, for where there is fire, there is hope. Sounds good anyway. Now if the good people of Narsarsuaq only had ethanol instead of gasoline for my fuel can. Ethanol is more environmentally-friendly, and it would not have made the air around me smell so much like my old lawn mower.

The wind fell off and rose up again, over and over as the night crept along. Oddly, or maybe not, by morning the fog hadn't cleared. *One more day,* I thought, lighting my stove for the seventeenth time in as many minutes.

In windy conditions maintaining a flame can be a chore, to put it mildly. I did have the option of just munching on some meusli and moving on down the trail; quick and easy, up and on my way. But if it hasn't become apparent by now, this trek was not about quick and easy. The physical goal, of course, was Qaqortoq. But the way there, the path taken, was the heart and soul of the trip.

Unfortunately it also came with wasted matches and dirty dishes.

I broke camp for the last time on this leg of my trek (or so I hoped). Then I threw my pack on my back and began walking into the wind.

Though it takes a little less time with each passing day, at the outset of a day's hike the legs need to reacquaint themselves with the idea of carrying more weight than usual over terrain that doesn't always lend itself to a smooth, steady gait. Today, on my last day before reaching Qaqortoq, my legs were quick to fall into a rhythm. The land, in turn, was quick to take them out with my first obstacle of the day: a three-meter cliff running off and out of sight in both directions. I looked over the ground below; crawling lazily across the land was the path I had lost.

Like that crack in the Earth the day before, there might, I thought, be an easier place to negotiate this cliff and move forward. No ladders in sight however, and really, three meters straight down is like stepping off the curb after a leap across the gaping gateway to the underworld. I dropped my hiking sticks down; they hit the soft ground with barely a whisper. This lends slight comfort to a ninety kilogram human being. I followed, landing not quite as softly though the ground was wonderfully forgiving. As I reached up with one pole and yanked on my pack straps, I thought about something I'd read about following marked trails on a trek. On the one hand it increases significantly your chances of survival. This merits a check in the positives column, no debate about it. But following a constantly guiding hand, it can scarcely be argued, takes away from the adventure. I wondered if I hadn't been striking a fair medium between these two as I hoisted my pack back up and walked on.

Time loses its meaning in the realm of my daydreams, and I realized I had no idea how much time had passed when I came upon a shepherd's hut in such a good state of repair that only the glaring lack of livestock gave the impression that it had been abandoned, and then only recently. I nudged open the door and glanced around at the neat, dark emptiness. I took out a pencil and scribbled my thoughts down. I flipped through the guestbook hanging on a nail inside the door, skimming through the few messages written in English and German. In this moment, more than at any other time on the trek (and in my life for that matter), I wished I could understand Danish. The feeling I got from people's words and a few scattered dates was that very few people actually come here to walk these fields, hills and fjords. I looked around. *No kidding.* The trekking guides I'd read said Greenland was a true hiking paradise. *Paradise,* I thought, sitting at home. I was sure there would be at least a few people trekking around. I couldn't find anyone in Vinska Gora to go with me, but no matter. I figured I would meet a smattering of fellow hikers along the way.

I looked across the land I'd just traversed. I was utterly alone. Alone in paradise. And I could only conclude that not everyone wants to go hiking in paradise. Not this version anyway. Perhaps it is only the rare individual who comes to a place such as this – for good or for bad. When I spoke to people who had come here before me, the concensus was obvious: that Greenland is truly special. Thus right from the beginning, thinking about my own trek, I didn't want to go to Nepal or South America. For my first trek, I wanted to take on the most demanding circumstances for my nascent capabilities. By doing so, future treks, whether alone or in company, would perhaps seem not so difficult. I envisioned approaching my physical and psychological limits, but not necessarily pushing them further and further forward on subsequent trips. It was a comical feeling, a good one. There would always be longer, steeper, bolder, more dangerous treks out there, but having neared my own limits here, maybe that would be enough. Maybe there'd be no compulsion to go any further. Or would there? This is one of those things that can only be answered over time. Weeks. Months. Years. For now I'd keep my sights set on Qaqortoq.

To my left I noticed a farm on a small island. I remember thinking at this moment how lonely a place like this, and life in a place like this, must be sometimes. The fields were neat if not manicured; I detected no hint of movement or life. It was a fair question if someone lived there at all anymore.

An ice-cold wind kicked up, whispering then rushing then howling through my ears. I felt a stinging in my cheeks. *Too prickly to be the cold.* On the ground in front of me, a thousand white dots bounced and scampered, all in the same direction. *Sleet?* This was a new and certainly unsolicited first. I took refuge in a meter-wide fissure in the rocky ground, warming up my last bits of soup with what turned out to be my final meal's worth of fuel. Now was not the time to walk into another mile-high wall of rock. The wind died down and I gulped down my soup and moved on. In minutes it seemed I was coming upon the (supposed) last shepherd's hut of the trail. This one was fully intact, and if someone told me it was their weekend cottage I probably would have believed them. Yet these huts belong to all people, locals and travelers alike. The food and drink on the shelves, unfortunately, do not. Pinned to the walls were curling posters of Greenland's impressive beauty, scenes that could make anyone want to be here in real life – though perhaps without the effort it takes to get here. I stepped back outside, the smell of the end of my trek growing stronger.

If Clemens and Niels were to be trusted, I figured I'd pretty much nailed down the correct pronunciation of Qaqortoq.

Much easier on the chords than Igaliku despite the abundance of q's. Thus I was breathing easy when a telecommunications tower suddenly appeared, rising high over the hills separating me from the southern tip of the land. I found it strange that I hadn't noticed it until that moment. This thought was immediately superseded by the realization that, through all my preparation and excitement and anticipation, I couldn't remember if I knew there would even *be* a telecommunications tower. Either way, it was now drawing me in, like the smell of mom's cooking after a long week of work. I broke into a jog, the weight on my back and in my legs suddenly gone. I ran up a grassy slope, faster it seemed than when I was making my life-or-death crevice jump. At the top of the hill I'm sure I caught a little air. And though my sights were set like lasers on the town below, my head was somewhere in the clouds. This is my best explanation for how I could lose the trail leading straight to the boarding house. But who in a moment like this can be bothered with such details?

I kept bounding forward; my legs felt rubbery, like on the last run of a long day of skiing. The descent to town seemed to drag on for hours. Then finally, and rather suddenly, I found myself face to face, nose to nose with the colored blocks and buildings of the largest town in southern Greenland: Qaqortoq. What a feeling! And it would be, quite literally, all downhill from here. Whatever successes my trek would bring me from this point on would be mere icing on the cake of my adventure. I walked quickly into town, my rucksack, my excitement, my satisfaction pushing me forward.

In minutes I was standing in front of a supermarket – one of the town's four, it was hard to fathom – surrounded by a loose crowd of about three dozen kids. They looked me over, another outsider come to trek across their land. Some of them began laughing; what for I would forever wonder. They spoke, but naturally I couldn't understand. They understood me though, and I hadn't even said anything. They waved as they walked over, a collective 'Don't worry we aren't here to rob you poor traveler' sort of gesture. Then they proceeded to grab and push and pull on me, all the way to the boarding house.

A quiet euphoria welled up inside me – and not simply for the realization that my stench was not driving these beautiful children away. What struck me was that this incredible feeling didn't spill out with a laugh or leak out in even a gentle smile, none that I could sense anyway. And I wondered for just a moment why not. I was tired, that was for certain. But was I so physically drained that I couldn't manage a kind expression? Throughout my trek deep feelings of elation and despondence, courage and frailty, confidence and caution and concern, would continue to ebb and flow in the deepest wellsprings of my soul. And here in Greenland, as in life, they would at times rise to the surface – but only in small amounts. I have never let my emotions flow freely; nor have I ever felt like I was purposely holding them back. They have always been there though, deep down; a small flame, an eternal flicker of a love for life, fed by lands as great as Greenland and things as small as a child's fingers, wrapped around my thumb. Yesterday and tomorrow, inside is where my emotions would be found. Today, in this moment, I would laugh with the children.

I'd barely dropped my pack on the floor before I was jumping feet first into the shower. I would have burned my clothes on the spot if I didn't still need them. Instead I took an easy stroll to the laundry room and washed away the residue of the trials of the past week. Then with everything dried and folded it was high time for some rest. *Blessed rest!* But the pain rising up in my little toe wouldn't allow it. In the shower I'd noticed how crushed and bloody it had become from all the walking. But it was only now, with the rest of my body relaxed, that the pain really started biting into me. The nail had also begun to cut into the skin of his neighbor, not wanting to be the only bloody one around. Oddly, in trying to somehow ease the discomfort, I found that it didn't hurt nearly as much if I was up walking around. A simple, effective prescription and, despite all the trekking, not all that unappealing either without that load on my back. So the question now before me was: Where to go on a Saturday night in Qaqortoq?

After a week of trekking the wide empty peninsula the town was as difficult as a refrigerator to navigate, and in minutes I had zeroed in on a piece of Greenland's nightlife, in the form of a clapboard discotheque. As the only foreigner in the place, and for no other reason I could possibly dream up, I found myself quite the attraction for the local girls. The novelty quickly turned ugly (in an admittedly compelling sort of way) as they made it quite clear without words they wanted to undress me down to my boxer shorts, right there at the bar. In Qaqortoq, the name of the apparent game is to drink yourself out of control as quickly and efficiently as possible, and let yourself go from there. In the midst of their hazy rompings I felt not the center of attention, but one who had simply walked into their alcohol-induced crossfire. Luckily (I suppose) the fire behind their antics fizzled out, and I stumbled back toward the hostel under the glint of the 4am dawn.

As physically spent as I was by now, it was still hard to miss the contrast between that lawless disco and the neat, proud school building next to the hostel. Perhaps it is due to a certain standard that Greenlanders hold themselves to (when not racing to pour drinks down their throats) that the students' rooms are remarkably clean and neat. Through the window the chairs, tables and desks appeared as precious artifacts, ordered and exact, free of juvenile images or etchings. There were no words or pictures scribbled on walls or in corners. I saw just one single piece of teenage human evidence, a sticker in the window, bearing the name of a popular Danish pop group.

Young children could always be expected to gather around the school, intrigued by any foreign presence but not so bold as to hang out in front of the hostel. The next day, when a trio of Germans arrived in town after trekking from Ittleq, the bigger kids walked beside them trying to match their long strides while the rest tumbled along behind. An older Englishman walked out into the street, and immediately a crowd of bubbling children gathered around him, holding out their pens so he could give them his autograph – on their hands. A few minutes later I followed him out and was swamped in a similar, beautifully childlike fashion.

Once they dispersed I looked around, soaking up the tranquil atmosphere of the capital of southern Greenland. Founded in 1775 by Norwegian merchants, the town was named after the Danish queen Juliane Julianehab. (The Danish still affectionately refer to this place as *Juliano*.) With 3500 residents, Qaqortoq is southern Greenland's biggest settlement. The majority live within the city proper – if there are in fact actual city limits – while the remaining three hundred or so live scattered across the surrounding hillsides and fields, small settlements of hardy folk minding a dozen sheep ranches and two reindeer farms.

Qaqortoq is quaint yet magnificently picturesque, a serene yet playful village situated between sea and lake, watched over by a cluster of mountains. The apartment blocks most people live in are clothed in modest colors, bright only against the barren backdrop of the land. On one balcony I spotted a pair of Elan skis, their RC-04 model from the 1980's. Quality and durability in a harsh environment; I shouldn't have been surprised. Elsewhere I spotted seal skins hung out to dry. The port was surrounded by small houses, one so tiny there had to be elves living there. I found three of the stores that qualified as supermarkets, at least in a Greenlandic sense. With some shops open every day of the year, one would think this was a full-fledged consumer society. In contrast to the seal skins still favored by some, there were also Gore-Tex jackets for sale –

mostly small, with a few mediums thrown in to add a patina of selection.

Relatively speaking, Qaqortoq also possesses a certain element of industry. A shipbuilding yard, though not a very large one, contains fairly modern facilities for producing and cutting fiberglass and polyester. There is also a tannery where seal skins are treated and the valuable fur separated. Not surprisingly, the fishing industry is alive and well, with Qaqortoq's port boasting the country's largest fountain, for whatever that is worth. The area is also decorated with rows of old homes, some of them more than two hundred years old. One houses a museum, rich with objects and artifacts testifying to the age-old Inuit way. The kayaks, harpoons, spears and other weapons on display were used by Greenland's native people as recently as fifty or sixty years ago. Also can be seen are traditional costumes and photographs of the Inuit past. Topping this off is Qaqortoq's open-air art exhibit titled 'Stone and Man.' After what I'd seen along my way, this seemed like a rather apropos theme.

In 1993 and 1994 Qaqortoq's summer days were filled with the squealing and grinding of machines. Underscoring the din was the banging of hammers and chisels and rock. A group of Scandinavian sculptors had decided to turn downtown into an outdoor art gallery, and each artist chose a boulder or rock and began carving out his ideas. For two summers inhabitants and visitors alike watched the transformation of these huge pieces of stone into works of art, the more than twenty finished pieces representing modern Greenlandic culture.

This art gallery under the skies served to brighten an otherwise cloudy, rainy afternoon as I strolled down to the lake on the west side of town. There I saw a group of young boys standing in a cirlce, wearing only swimsuits. One after another they slapped hands and laughed and ran and jumped into the ten-degree water. Watching them, my own hands dug deep into my pockets, the chill I'd almost forgotten about returned to my bones.

Like every other town in Greenland, Qaqortoq maintains a soccer field – though surfaced with sand, not grass. As in most of the rest of the world, soccer enjoys a fair bit of popularity here. As far as I could ascertain, Greenland would readily put a team together and join FIFA if they only had a place where they could practice year-round. Until that day arrives, they will continue rooting for Denmark. Still, they take pride in their coach, the reknowned Dane Sepp Piontek, and can revel in their historic 4-1 victory over Tibet in a friendly match held in Denmark on June 30, 2001. Today the soccer field was deserted, but from what I heard the locals put it to good use when the weather cooperates.

A common misconception about summiting Mt. Everest is that a whole lot happens at the top. But those who have been there will tell you a different story: a moment to revel in making it to the roof of the world, a quick snapshot or two and you start heading right back down that mountain. The top is only the halfway point. There's no time for a picnic.

Likewise, my final stroll around Qaqortoq the next morning felt nothing short of surreal. The months of planning, all the preparation, the work and the wonder and the worrying. The long, hard, brilliant trek to get here, all the anxiety and the anticipation; suddenly it was all over, time to board a postal ferry for the day-long trip to the 'neighboring' settlement of Nanortalik.

At the outset the skies were cloudy, which detracts not one bit from the beauty of the icebergs. These bergs break off of glaciers on the eastern coast of Greenland and drift around the cape and along the western seaboard for as long as they don't melt or wend into the fjords. Despite the gloomy heavens we were blessed with calm seas, making for as favorable conditions as anyone can hope for in this slice of the world.

Stopping in port at each settlement on our route was a veritable social event. Workers on board the ship hauled mail and goods to the post office and the shops nearby. A few passengers disembarked while others got on – by ladder, which meant an adventure for the older folk. We were often docked for a half hour or more, and I used this time to hustle off and explore what I could of each village. In some I came upon greenhouses for growing such things as potatoes and cabbage. In a few I sensed a suspicion of foreigners in the air. There was no twinkle in the children's eyes; I was regarded with deliberate indifference. Still, I left thinking it was good to have been there.

As we plied the water between stops, hunters showed off their boating skills and their bravado, coming within inches of colliding with our lumbering vessel then buzzing off again. I held my breath each time one of them came at us, waiting for disaster to strike, wondering if there were any laws around here. On board I met a young man who claimed to be associated with Greenland's national women's handball team. ('I didn't know there was one,' I said.) He spoke very good English – certainly enough to put me to shame – and helped us both while away the time by relating odd bits about Greenland to me. He said he liked to go out and hunt polar bear every now and then, not far from Nanortalik. *'They ride the current down the east coast into the southern regions,'* he explained. I pictured a group of polar bears hanging out on ice floes, cruising along the shore. *'Look over there,'* he blurted out a few moments later, pointing out a small settlement tucked in between the water and the rocks. *'That little gray building is an alcohol treatment center.'* I squinted and looked for the disco.

The skies cleared as we rolled into the afternoon, unveiling serrated mountains rising up from the distant horizon. I'd seen pictures of these peninsular peaks, with the mighty Kirkespiret rising highest among them. As with any place of beauty, there is nothing like being there. Even miles away. Buried in the land at their feet, my friend told me, they'd recently discovered gold. The idea was a delight to ponder, this amazing land bestowing such a windfall upon the natives. The feeling, however, was short-lived. *'Greenlanders,'* my friend explained, *'are sadly under-educated in terms of business and capitalism. They gain very little from their own mining activity.'* This because the excavated ore leaves Greenland in the form it was found, the extraction processes then carried out in Spain. I felt myself hoping the locals would wisen up before a group of outsiders figured out how to overcome the logistical difficulties involved in excavating the enormous mineral wealth believed to be lying beneath Greenland's protective ice.

As afternoon bled into evening we motored into the harbor of the southernmost commune of all Greenland, Nanortalik. Niels from the local tourist office (not to be confused with Niels from Copenhagen) was there on the dock waiting for me and two Frenchmen who had also been on board. We shook hands and piled into his large off-road vehicle for a quick tour of the town, and in the first quiet moment I asked this new friend of mine what the real deal was with polar bears in Greenland.

'Actually, just two years ago,' he readily offered, *'three of them were shot right near here.'* Then he added something about a hunter from nearby Ammassalik bagging a bear two days ago. Our driver and guide then went on to talk about how and when the Danes founded Nanortalik, mentioning in quiet passing that we didn't have to keep our seatbelts fastened. This struck me not only as out of place but also pointedly unnerving. What, exactly, was he preparing us for?

We drove past a church and a rocky boulder in the shape of a man's head, apparently Knud Rasmussen, the famous Arctic researcher. Following this was a wonderfully restored house in Old Nanortalik, which turned out to be our small and very comfortable hostel. Perfect, as I felt quite ready for a few quiet moments after listening to the rumble of the ferry all day.

Without any hesitation or ceremony I dropped my rucksack on my bed, then headed for the kitchen and put a pot of water on the stove. I found a box of peppermint tea, and fell so deeply into the process of filtering and boiling my water I didn't notice the whale breaching the waters of the sea outside.

Niels slapped me on the shoulder. *'What are you, British? Put down the tea and look outside!'* Suddenly I was fighting the Frenchmen for space in the one tiny window in the room. *'That's a minke whale,'* Niels said, pointing. *'There are killer whales out in the open sea; the minkes come inland to hide from them.'* This, I thought, was quite clever for an animal called a minke.

With Niels's assistance I arranged to meet the hunter from Aappilattoq that the Niels from Copenhagen had first put me in touch with. If the weather agreed, this man (not named Niels) would take me by speedboat to Lindenow Fjord along the eastern side of Greenland. I had read during my research into Greenland that Tommelfinger, rising more than two thousand meters from the waters of Lindenow, was considered by some to be the most beautiful mountain on the planet. Add to this a fjord full of icebergs and ice floes, steep waterfalls, hidden ruins and glaciers with their tongues in the sea, and you have more than ample reason to pay a hard-earned visit to this, the most distant settlement of southern Greenland. Luckily I was able to negotiate with the hunter – via e-mail of all things – to where I could afford the trip.

Seeking out my Inuit ruins remained another matter.

In the hostel I ran into a Swedish couple that had been on my flight into Greenland; they had just trekked across the Narsaq Peninsula. I also met three rock climbers from the Czech Republic; they had their sights set on the mountain known as Ketil, aiming to conquer the most famous rock wall in all of southern Greenland. They spoke with fervor about how exhilarating it felt to be hanging from a wall of rock as the wind whipped all around – a feeling I was not quite familiar with as I have always made it a point to never find myself clinging to an immense and very vertical piece of rock in any weather. I could well imagine the scene, though, and as they spoke I thought about the desolation of Greenland contrasting with the famous and well-populated El Capitan rockface in Yosemite, California. Where would be the better place to find oneself clinging to an immense rock wall?

For me the answer is simple: No.

The South of Greenland offers numerous demanding rock climbs for the interested unzipped soul, many of them as yet unconquered. There are mountains in Greenland also awaiting their first successful summiter. Some may forever remain that way. I, on the other hand, prefer to keep my adventures more horizontal. Planning my trek through this land I wanted to hike to Cape Farewell, the southernmost tip of Greenland. This, I believed, was a place more beautiful than any human being could rightfully imagine. The path I was looking at started by running past a huge lake, leading to where Greenland's flora is purportedly at its richest. Climbing slowly out of a valley, the path would lead up into a vast swath of glaciers and mountains, views of the forest green fjords below waiting take your breath away. After crossing a plateau a steep descent would bring you back down to the foot of the mountains and back around to where the trail began.

When I met this Danish couple, in my hostel in Narsarsuaq, they told me they were going to make this trek. Meeting them again there in Nanortalik, I suspected that something had gone wrong. With a polite reacquainting and a little gentle prodding they told me what had happened.

'As the trail winds past the lake it becomes overgrown with shrubs.' Thus progress was very slow and difficult, particularly on the uphill. They'd given up after two days, *'saved from our trekking hell by a local who happened by in his boat.'* Besides the thick overgrowth they had fought the wind and the rain throughout those two days, making the entire experience a wet, cold, miserable one. Greenland, while indescribably beautiful, can indeed be a cruel, unforgiving place. Sometimes she refuses even to provide a place to pitch a tent, allowing one only a pile of creaking, shifting rocks. When a storm hits unexpectedly, fierce enough to drive you off the land, help is not always readily available. Imagine waiting an entire day in the driving, freezing rain for a ride home, nary a Starbuck's to duck into and thirty wet kilograms on your back. Not long before I arrived in Greenland a hunter got caught in a wild storm and had to take refuge at the base of a cliff. Fortunately he only had to wait twenty-four hours before being found. One thin shiny space blanket was all that kept him safe from major frostbite and, possibly, away from death's reach.

Out here there is not much separation between good luck and hard luck. Success and failure. Life and death. I looked back at my casual preparedness. My inexperience and my carelessness. A respect for this place seeped back into me, a feeling that was so very strong, and is still near impossible to put into words.

TO AAPPILATTOQ, THE END OF THE WORLD

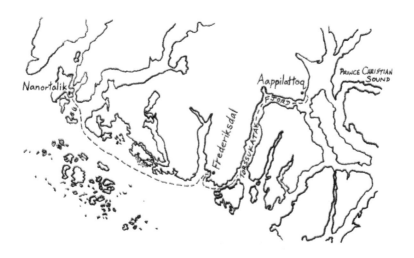

The southernmost region of Greenland, known by the locals as Uummanarsuaq, was by all evidence formed during the last Ice Age. Massive glaciers pushed irresistably southward, carving immense valleys through the mountains fronting the North Atlantic. These were the beginnings of the deep, narrow fjords we see today. As our ferry plowed steadily toward this magical place I entertained visions of walking in the grandest of all gardens; of surveying the land and the sea from the highest peaks around. These images were quickly and quite rudely split in half by a Dane (by this time I figured it was safe to assume) with a leer in his eye and beer on his breath.

'Aappilattoq?' He leaned against the railing and stared at me, waiting for an answer if that was really a question. 'God-willing,' I said, unable to come up with a good one-word response and settling for a hyphenated two. 'Cape Farewell?' I grinned. 'You bet.' He shook a finger at me. 'Go see Cape Horn first.' It was a little late for that but he was unfazed, firmly asserting that I or anyone else who thinks Cape Horn is the most wildly beautiful place on Earth is sadly mistaken. Actually I'd never seen either of them. I wondered how many people have actually seen both – and if the Brewmaster now standing between me and my view was one of them. The only distinction I could aptly make between the two was that Cape Farewell is visited by far fewer people – certainly not a reliable barometer for measuring the relative beauty of anything. 'After you see Cape Horn, then come out to Cape Farewell.' Only in this way, he swore, might I not be so disappointed with Cape Horn.

I nodded in agreement and looked over his shoulder, out at the choppy water. The afternoon wind was already whipping up, warning of harsher weather to come. Our ship lurched and pitched in slow motion. My saucy friend tapped my arm with his beer, offering his friendly and wholly unsolicited advice. 'Swing with the boat,' he said, swaying side to side. 'Keeps you from getting seasick.' I figured if it worked for him it had to work for me. 'Thanks for the tip.' I looked around the boat in vain for another foreigner. *'I'm Tomas,'* he said, offering his hand – which had an unopened beer in it. *'Here. A little bit of protection against the weather.'* I thanked him and slid the can into my coat pocket.

From there he went on to explain how he was employed at the weather station in Prince Christian Sound. Oddly, he didn't seem all that interested in his own words, his aloof manner directed more toward the banks of the fjord sliding slowly past. But then his voice brightened as he began to explain how the waters freeze enough from time to time to attract polar bears – which the people tend to enjoy killing. When the weather is amicable they fill their snowmobiles with gas and load up their guns and head off across the whitened land. *'It's a damn good time,'* he said like I might not believe him.

While interesting enough in the context of life on Greenland, hunting was not at the top of my list of preferred conversations, and I gently steered Tomas instead toward the idea of finding accommodation in Aappilattoq. *'Sure, I can help you with that,'* he said, a glimmer in his mostly glazed eyes. *'There's a place in town you can stay at for a hundred Danish Crowns. Or...'* He pointed, at me or maybe at the beer in my pocket. *'There's another option, for backpackers looking for much cheaper boarding.'* I waited. He waited. I shrugged and raised my eyebrows. *'You can bunk up with us at the weather station – in exchange for a good strong bottle.'* Tomas grinned and went on about the various kinds of libations they already had on hand: beer, wine, whiskey, even champagne in addition to the long list of non-alcoholic drinks which he also began

101

checking off out loud. *'But we could use better spirits,'* he explained, not actually explaining what better spirits were. He then went on to talk about how he missed his normal life, not least of all his wife and three children who were back in Denmark. But the generous wages kept him working – and drinking – in Greenland.

The lasting impression Tomas left me with came when I told him about my plans to go to Lindenow Fjord with a local hunter, as long as the weather improved. To make a check on the forecast, I asked him if I could drop by the weather station. *'Sure, stop on by,'* he said. *'But don't bother bringing along any lousy Inuit.'* As if to drive his point home, whatever it was, he showed me on a map where the Inuit are not allowed to catch salmon and which rivers, in their own country, they may fish. Twenty minutes later, alone again, I wondered if these fishing laws were real or just fanciful wishing on the part of one disgruntled, burping outsider.

With the wind growing stronger our ship remained close to shoreline. The mountains on our left, a thousand meters high, stood half-hidden in the clouds. The sea grew restless, tossing whitecaps around. After three hours we made a welcome stop in the southern settlement of Frederiksdal.

Consisting of a semicircle of buildings lining a natural amphitheater tucked into the feet of the granite mountains, Frederiksdal had to be the most attractive settlement I'd seen to this point. In the middle of the village stood a red Moravian church, one hundred and fifty years old by most accounts. The colorful houses stretched away on both sides, arcing around, giving them all a wonderful view of the painted wooden pride of their town. The pier, the traditional center of any settlement, was in this case outside the actual center of the village. The traffic along the only road consisted of a single pickup truck, transporting everyone and all their belongings back and forth.

From Frederiksdal we slipped through a narrow passage and into Torsukattak Fjord. August ice floes swam lazily in the dark water, silent beneath the steep walls of the surrounding brown-gray mountains. The strengthening wind gradually drove everyone inside, and I watched from a window the dancing, spraying waterfalls cascading over the light blue glaciers and down the steep faces of those sawtooth mountains. A scattering of seals lazed in the water, watching sleepily everything going on around them. I ventured back outside, determined to shoot a few good photos in spite of the wind now blowing salt water all over everyone and everything. I wiped my wet face with one wet hand; the weather, though irritating, wouldn't hurt me. But my camera wasn't going to tolerate much of this abuse. The ferry dipped and rose with the restive waters. Inside, two hard and heavy plastic containers dropped six feet to the floor, the heart-stopping banging plunging the crowd of passengers into a moment of stunned silence.

But perhaps the hours of unease was the right and proper introduction to Aappilattoq and the end of the world. Jörg, God bless him, was waiting for me on the pier, smile dripping with smug satisfaction. *'You thought I might not come?'* he said. I slapped him on both shoulders. 'Never doubted it!' And he led me to the home of his new fiancee, giddy in anticipation of dinner: his favorite dish, the indispensible Danish potato plate. Yet all the while he's grumbling about the Inuits' trademark forgetfulness. *'They remember slowly and forget quickly,'* he said as he walked up the short steps and opened the door to a modest one-story home. Without slowing his step he walked across the living room and ducked through a small doorway. I followed, not knowing what else to do.

An apron made of gray and black seal skin hung from a nail on the far kitchen wall. In one corner the aroma of dried fish wafted up. In another corner were two pairs of waterproof boots, along with a couple of hunting rifles. Jörg introduced me to dark-haired, dark-eyed Daniel, the head of the household, and the various members of his family, including Blendine, Daniel's sister and Jörg's fiancee. As I was the first traveler to ever set foot in Daniel's house, a calmly momentous occasion, everyone came together to tip a glass. And what better to toast with than Greenland's very own beer, brewed in the capital of Nuuk from a Danish recipe.

Daniel was a teacher who spoke very good English. *'But I still hunt from time to time,'* he explained in between sips. Daniel soon drifted onto the subject of survival on Greenland, lamenting how *'so-called green pacifists like Greenpeace'* were making life more and more difficult for him and his people. Greenpeace, he grumbled, destroyed the seal skin trade in Greenland by making the boorish mistake of likening Inuit dependence on seal for subsistence to the cruel killing of young white seal pups in Canada for sport (he used far fewer words to say so). *'Are you a Greenpeace supporter?'* he asked. I tried to step lightly. 'I'm against killing seal puppies for fun.' I shifted my eyes and the subject. 'So where is Peter?'

Daniel put his beer down. *'Peter is in Nanortalik.'* I almost choked on my beer. 'In Nanortalik?' I had already arranged to have him take me to Lindenow Fjord. *'Oh, yeah,'* Daniel said easily. *'School starts next week.'* So there went my trip to Lindenow – unless Daniel would agree to take me. *'Of course,'* he said, much to my delight and relief. *'Peter and I are the only ones with boats suitable for the trip. But the weather right now is making it impossible to leave the harbor.'* A guest in their home, drinking their beer, I decided to drop the subject.

We fell into lighter, more jovial conversation for the next couple of hours, the effects of the alcohol beginning to show on everyone's faces. Jörg was translating what everyone else was saying, regardless of whether it was in Inuit or in English. When my stomach started grumbling I asked Daniel if he had a bit of gas. His face turned sober for a moment. The others stared in surprise. Was this bit of slang universal? 'I need gas for my stove,' I explained. By this time Daniel was too drunk to answer in English, so he showed me with his hands how he didn't want me blowing up his house. With my own gestures I assured him that nothing would go *boom*. But the point was moot either way; he had none, and the stores in the village all closed at 4pm. To compensate I was offered the use of Jörg's fiancee's tiny home, a prefabricated structure with no heat, electricity or hot water for the moment. Blendine had recently been diagnosed with cancer and had just returned from a treatment session in Copenhagen, and so was staying there in

Daniel's house. The electricity had been shut off since she left, though that wouldn't make much difference during the long summer days. And I could fetch water from one of the many outdoor taps around the village. With a strong wind blowing for three days, though, living without heat might be a minor trial. Still, it beat a damp tent in a rocky field. Their living room would have done just fine but I decided not to ask.

My new home consisted of a single room with two large windows. The old kitchenette had a few dishes, a gas cooker with no gas and a creaky table with four chairs. There was even a small toilet near the entrance which, after a week in the wild, was pretty exciting. The wind and rain would not be getting to me tonight. I smiled, put my rucksack down and returned to Daniel's place. I made dinner and ate with his children. Then, over another beer, Jörg explained to me why he had really come to Greenland.

I'm kind of hiding from the Danish authorities, he said, having killed a fox (an immensely important one I had to surmise) and committed a few other offenses back home. He also said he had been married six times. This I found even more difficult to believe. But he ignored my expression and carried on, telling me how he didn't plan on actually marrying Blendine because he didn't want to be put through another divorce. He showed me pictures of some of his former wives, particularly proud of one beautiful girl from Ammassalik. He talked about these things with Blendine right there; she understood every word. She also bragged about how she once slipped out of bed and stole away to a neighbor's house early one morning. Jealous Jörg went out looking for her, but by the time he saw her again it was already too late. Blendine accused Jörg of being the village gigolo, with most of the young women in town under his thumb. But then she admitted how many men she herself had slept with. This, I guessed, was life at the end of the world.

The wind outside whistled and howled. Rain began pelting the windows. As I lay on Blendine's floor I wondered where I would be if I hadn't had the good fortune of walking the wrong way from the Narsarsuaq airport and running into Jörg. What might have happened if I had ended up alone, walking through this unpredictable land? Where would I have camped? *How* would I have camped? How would I cook my dinner, pitch my tent, or have the slightest hope of having a dry square inch to wear or rest upon? Even if I knew what better spirits were there was no getting to the weather station, for me or for Tomas. All I would have was a suspicious reference to paying one hundred Kroner per night somewhere.

I thought about these things as I sank deeper into my warm dry sleeping bag.

But I didn't fall asleep easily, even inside, what with the instability of the elements outside. Eventually, I would have to continue on out there. For hours it didn't seem like I'd so much as dozed off. Yet I managed to hibernate until nine the next morning. I walked over to Daniel's house to make myself my usual simple breakfast; when his wife Terine saw me at work in her kitchen she rushed off to the market without a word and came back with some corn flax. Then she proceeded to copy everything I was doing. Daniel picked up his guitar and began to strum and sing. One of the neighbors came up to the house and walked right through the door, carrying a two-liter plastic bottle a quarter full of homemade liquor. In a peculiar sort of reverse Halloween he was walking from house to house sharing his nectar and toasting to everyone's happiness. Daniel took a thick mouthful. I only touched my tongue to the suspicious liquid. At first I only sensed a bitter bite; but then I made the mistake of breathing in, and in a flash my throat was on fire.

The adults began singing together. The coffee table was soon covered with beer cans. We were having a grand old time...until Daniel's sister Rebekka stormed into the house and started spouting off about everyone sitting around drinking in the presence of this poor traveller, particularly so early in the day. Did she not notice I was having a grand old time myself? The beer cans were quickly replaced with cups of coffee and tea, the atmosphere quickly sobering. Time passed quickly. People emerged from the shop one by one holding bags full of cans of beer. Several children stopped by the house, gazing intently at the sight and shape of the foreigner in front of them.

'Our children are adopted,' Daniel told me, as they were unable to have children of their own. 'In Greenland children belong as much to the community as to their parents. If you can't have children of your own you might expect to be given one or two as birthday gifts.'

What??? I couldn't fathom the idea. But it obviously made perfect sense to Daniel. 'You never know when you might need *your neighbor's help.'* This is one way they maintained solid relationships with each other. Later we took a 'family' photo together, as I was indeed feeling like one of Daniel's own.

In the afternoon I thought I could use a little peace and quiet. (Imagine that, after all those days of hiking in solitude.) I roamed the village, searching for a decent place to pitch a tent in this rocky, pebbly, stone-infested land. And where would I ever find solid ground for a few geometrically-aligned tent pegs? After a while of wandering I found a level swath of grass and dirt, good enough (barely) for a few quiet hours outdoors.

But somehow Tomas found me and settled in uninvited for a chat. The glazed look in his eyes now replaced with mere fatigue, he seemed overly excited about the instant coffee I made him. Then he continued his rant from the day before, railing away on the Inuit way of life: no hotels, no inns, no night life...nothing. He had spoken with his co-worker at the weather station; he'd be coming to get Tomas as soon as the weather allowed. Until then he would be paying a hundred crowns per night for the only option in town, which was not a hostel but rather a kind of nursing home, complete with a real nurse. I doubted they accepted booze for payment.

Jörg and Blendine came by after a while. Blendine told me a night of accommodation in my tiny home would be a hundred and fifty Danish Kroner. 'It can't be that much,' I protested as politely as I could, what with the lack of heat, water and electricity. I could have all of that for less down the street at the nursing home. Plus I'd get a nurse for free. We soon agreed on fifty per night. Then as a show of thanks I bought them some beer. Daniel invited me to dinner that evening. Terine fired up a pot of unbelievable fish soup. Bellies full, Daniel then invited me to spend the night in his warm, comfortable home; I didn't waste much time accepting. Apparently they were convinced I was not a Greenpeace supporter and thus not a dangerous man.

With the evening came a fair bit of alcohol, as I expected. But I didn't figure on Daniel and Jörg getting into an argument so heated they would come to fisticuffs. Fortunately everyone else was already in bed. Plus Daniel was too tipsy to put up much of a fight and didn't make it past the first round. Soon they calmed down and we all hit the sack, me wondering what the nurse looked like.

Finally, on my third day at the end of the world, the winds showed signs of dying down. But the waters were still roiling; Daniel's boat wouldn't stand a chance. So what else to do but go for a walk?

Naturally, the pier is Aappilattoq's door and window to the world. Here, as in most places, it is also the focus of daily life, with the supermarket, bank and post office nearby. Available in the market are, among other things, bullets (indispensible for efficient seal-hunting) and, for the size of the town, a rather impressive selection of adult videos. In the geographical center of Aappilattoq stands a protestant church, along with a school the children attend through sixth grade. If they continue with their schooling they go to Nanortalik. There are no cars in the village, though the town boasts two yellow bulldozers. I looked around. Not a pile of dirt out of place. I could barely speculate as to the necessity of a pair of earthmovers here at the end of the world. Someone would explain to me later that they used to only have one, but it broke down and no one knew how to fix it so they got another one.

This would clear up half of the incongruity.

In the afternoon a crew of Poles and Czechs sailed into the harbor in a motorless wooden ship. Striking up a conversation with the friendly bunch, I learned they were in the midst of a sort of Viking reenactment. Setting sail from Denmark, they stopped off in the Faroe Islands on their way to Iceland. From there they headed for the east coast of Greenland and made their way around the cape. They would finish their voyage upon landing on the shores of Canada.

Thirty miles off the Greenland coast they had encountered their first bergs and floes, but without incident were able to navigate through to the fjords of Prince Christian Sound and into Aappilattoq. They took a shot at goading some of the locals into sailing with them, but the Inuit can seem an exceptionally cautious people. I bid them good luck and left them still trying. Perhaps they found an adventurous soul, though I'm sure I'll never know.

In Aappilattoq, more than anywhere else to that point along my journey, I sensed an enduring pride in the living traditions of Greenland – and the weighty proposition of relying and subsisting on nature. While the people lived in modern houses, not in igloos, the men still hunted seal for their skins, fur and meat. In winter they also ventured off in search of polar bears along the the desolate eastern side of this, the largest island in

111

the world. Yet the Internet has also found its way to this remote place. Daniel hadn't the slightest clue about computers, but Peter was basically the IT guy for the village.

The people of Aappilattoq were quick to win over my heart. Within hours of my windswept arrival the news had made it to every pair of ears around that there was a traveller in town – *'from the peaceful part of the Balkans'* as Tomas quaintly described it. During my time in Aappilattoq I was barely able to visit all the kind people who had approached me in their spirited humility to invite me into their homes. Some of them had come from places far east of Greenland. Others spoke of their Mongol ancestry, or of native North American Indian lineage. I'd also heard that approximately a third of the town could claim some degree of European blood. This may have been the end of the world, but the world, indeed, is round.

I said goodbye to Tomas late in the afternoon, his co-worker at the weather station finally able to maneuver his zodiac through Prince Christian Sound. He invited me to go along. I told him I didn't have any good spirits. He shrugged and turned away.

That evening, my last in Aappilattoq, Daniel turned on the TV. And what was on? A documentary about Viking ruins in Greenland and the life of Erik the Red. Daniel didn't care so much for the program, he said he just wanted to show me that not only did they have a TV, but they were able to watch real programs. Life on Greenland is still to a degree a struggle for survival though, and there isn't a whole lot of time for soap operas. With images of Viking ruins floating in the background of our conversation, I felt that I was in for something special that next day.

Before the evening had moved too far along a small group of sturdy-looking men showed up to talk to Karli, Rebekka's son. I'd noticed these men earlier that afternoon, outside cleaning fishing nets. Though everyone was speaking Inuit I thought I could pretty much figure what they were talking about. So I didn't say a word as we all went to bed quite early.

The boys got up at four in the morning to load up their boats. They were not going fishing on this day, but seal hunting. Terine was already up, scrubbing and cleaning a seal skin on a rock in front of the house. Being the one on vacation, I went out and did my own thing, taking more pictures of the many sides and angles of Aappilattoq.

Under the glow of the early morning sun the village really showed off its beauty. The sight – the experience of seeing this place in such a light – hammered home the feeling that I was in a truly unique place. I climbed the grassy slopes rising up behind the settlement. The blue-green waterways surrounding the village on three sides sparkled in the morning. Although the wind had blown away my plans to see Lindenow Fjord and any outlying Inuit ruins and remains, I found fair consolation in having the time to see, listen to, taste and thus to garner a clearer understanding of the ongoing life of the Inuit. Long after I would say my good-byes, the hope would stay with me that I would return to dig deeper into the spirit of this place.

Even as I write I feel a tangible yearning to go back. Perhaps I left a part of me behind. Maybe I simply want more for myself.

Either way, Aappilattoq has something unnamable, something so humanly fundamental that once it seeps into your soul you feel richer somehow, more complete. On a less esoteric note, I had the great privilege of meeting some wonderful people who would, if I ever made it back, take me to their hunting cabins while they went out on one of their polar bear hunts – in a place, they say, where can be found the most beautiful waterfalls in Greenland, the most breath-taking mountains, wildly warm lakes and long-abandoned dwellings. These alone are enough to coax me back to the end of the world. The profound feeling of wealth and satisfaction that Aappilattoq offers is just the icing on the cake – though perhaps digging into the cake itself is the source of this indescribable feeling.

Travel in the Arctic is quite different from travel in places where there are roads. On the road, things are more predictable. Your destinations are more accessible, your goals more easily achieved. In this sense everything I saw, each place I reached, came with a dose of quiet gratification. So while I might have been disappointed at having missed out on something I wanted to see, it was not for lack of effort. The Arctic doesn't care when you want to go where, so in the end you have to be satisfied with what the she throws at you, and from this eke out your own version of a beautiful vacation.

The time had come to say goodbye to my friends. The moment was enough to merit Terine putting down her semi-circular knife and taking a break from her incessant scraping and cleaning of seal skins. I put out my hand. She slapped it away and hugged me like I was her son, off on a trek to the other end of the world.

At the pier the ferry was already full, as it was time for the older children to head to Nanortalik and their boarding school. It was only the middle of August, but classes would start that following Monday. Practically the entire village had descended on the pier to wave goodbye and wish the kids well, particularly those who were leaving home for the first time. It was an emotional moment, one of those special times where you see people at their most genuine.

Our boat groaned and pulled away; the water widened; and soon the village disappeared into the mist. The past few days had been more than I could hope for, Lindenow or not. Yet I felt my mind quickly turning toward the beauty of Torssukatak Fjord. We passed the Polish-Czech expedition along the way back to Frederiksdal, where we took on still more passengers – most of them students going through the same parting ritual I'd just witnessed in Aappilattoq. As we pulled out into the open water again I struck up a conversation with a European-looking man standing nearby. 'What are you doing here in Greenland?' (Indeed the standard opener for any conversation between two white guys.) He told me he was from Denmark – surprise surprise – and explained he was out there on a project mounting beacons so commercial ships as well as the locals could better, more safely navigate the fjords in stormy weather. This wasn't the first time I got the impression the person in front of me was only there to make a quick buck. Later on, as punishment from the pagan gods for thinking such thoughts about people I barely knew, I discovered I had lost a roll of film and along with it a veritable chapter of photographic memories of Aappilattoq. For what it was worth, I reminded myself the experience of being there would always remain in my mind and my heart. Still, I tried to keep my thoughts more forgiving.

Four hours of calm seas later, my mind had moved on, and we were drifting along the shores of Nanortalik, the 'place of polar bears.'

NANORTALIK

Upon arrival I set out for the tourist office to drop in on Niels. After a hearty handshake and a round of questions about my time in Aappilattoq, I asked him to point me toward a spot of ground where I could camp. *'Pick a lake,'* he said, meaning one of the many surrounding the town. *'Then pitch your tent so you are facing historical Nanortalik.'*

He then started in about the very special event going on in town that very next day – an occasion centered around the beginning of the school year, something I was fast becoming acquainted with. *'The Saturday before is always a lively good time, Damjan. Your timing is perfect!'*

Rather than the dockside farewell routine I'd seen in Aappilattoq and Frederiksdal, here in Nanortalik there would be a ceremony of admission of newcomers to the elementary school, a ritual attended by the entire village, many dressed up in traditional Greenlandic garb. This trekker, of course, would have to try to blend in wearing dirty hikers and Gore-Tex.

Another warm handshake and I left Niels to find a home among the quiet lakes lining the edges of town.

In the morning I got up extra early to take in the local fish market, the true heart and soul of any town or village that has one. Tables, buckets and boxes sat in crooked stacks and rows, overloaded with freshly-caught fish alongside samples of seal meat and entrails. The pungent aroma permeated the air and my nostrils. Watery blood and bits of marine flesh splattered and squished underfoot. My senses were intrigued – and very soon saturated. I promised myself I would return after the day's festivities to pick up some fresh catch and prepare myself a nice Greenlandic seafood meal over a campfire.

Rolling up to the school I saw that a fair group of parents had already gathered. More than a few of them were decked out in their national costumes. I shuffled my boots, trying to wipe away the mud and shreds of tissue.

The traditional female costume is beautifully intricate, silk or cotton colored a rich crimson, embroidered in bright colors across the chest and shoulders and on down to the elbows. The thick black collar is made from seal skin, as are their pants, richly laced and decorated down to their deerskin boots.

The ceremony began with the incoming students filing onto the stage. (Cute as kids in uniform I'd have to say.) They were greeted by the school's headmaster and each of them was given a Greenlandic flag. With the top half white, representing the icecap over Greenland, and the bottom half red to represent the deep fjords (though to that point I hadn't seen any red fjords), the flag has the same color scheme as the Danish flag. In the middle lies a circle, the lower white half an abstract image of an iceberg, the top red half combining with the white to symbolize the polar day and night.

At one point, after no signal I could ascertain, people in the crowd suddenly began chucking coins onto the stage. In a flash the children were throwing their uniformed selves all over the floor, fighting each other for these tokens of good luck. Soon thereafter, the kids rattled and disheveled, the ceremony ended and the crowd slowly dispersed. I went back to the fish market, more intrigued than hungry, though this was soon irrelevant as the market had already shut down for the day. So I decided on the only other point of particular intrigue Nanortalik had to offer and headed south.

The Danish conquerors of the late 18th Century were said to have established several settlements in the area, one on the southern part of Nanortalik Island. I walked the hills and down toward the shoreline, in search of these relatively young and modest remains. Scattered around were the foundations of buildings of a few varying shapes and sizes; some could have been people's homes, others the tradesmen's shops. One might well have served as a communal hall. A meter-high white cross stood listing in the rocky ground where the church once stood. Remains of graves were also evident, a poignant sight in any land but somehow thick with added significance in a place that has seen entire cultures come and go.

Nowadays the site takes on a different sort of relevance with the tourist crowds that come and go.

The sleek white monster was floating offshore when I got back to town. She was a real behemoth, at least a hundred meters long, anchored out in deeper waters. Her passengers whizzed toward shore in small groups on high-speed outboard zodiacs. These tourists would stay in town for all of three hours. Many of them did little to hide their displeasure as they scanned the streets and houses, their noses slightly, perceptibly turned up in response to the dirt roads and odd bits of trash they'd come all this way to see. The town must have looked nothing less than a garbage dump to the fastidious Germans, approving only of the inside of the tiny church. *'Sauber, sauber,'* they mumbled to themselves and each other as they milled around in the dim light, half dead compared to the one man with the camera and tripod racing in and out of them. If I were their tour guide I'd be tempted to let them sulk there in the church until it was time for them to ship off and go grumble about their next stop.

In contrast to the rest of the town, which certainly isn't a dump by any means, Old Nanortalik is picture-perfect. Small homes sit neatly about, well-kept if not overtly ornate. Offered as an open-air museum, there are still turf houses, tents made from seal skins, and umiak, boats larger than kayaks, used primarily as transportation for women and children. Gathered in this special part of town is the architectural heritage of Greenland's Inuit and Danish past, the former inhabitants now living in apartment blocks in town. As I roamed amidst the German tourists – *'sauber, sauber, ja...'* – some local hunters reached in and grabbed me, separating me from the surly herd.

They had me sit with them. They offered me beer. They spoke to me with what little English they knew, garnered from the occasional open-water boat tours they would offer to tourists. Wanting to reciprocate my new friends' goodwill, I ran over to the supermarket and bought a few cans of beer to add to the party. We managed some conversation and some good laughs; we launched a signal rocket, just for kicks. Whatever the reason they picked me out of the crowd, I was heartily grateful. A couple Carlsbergs fuller, I thanked my comrades and excused myself to continue my stroll around town.

I stumbled upon a kiosk where I could get some kebab; a pleasant shock, as I'd never seen kebab in Slovenia. Looking around at the locals and their fancy boots I'd also say fashion makes it here to the remote islands of Greenland before finding its way to Ljubljana. Kebab and fashion. What did this country not have? As afternoon turned to evening I watched a Danish freighter sail into the harbor. And for the first time I witnessed Greenlanders moving faster than a glacier, for they only had so much time to unload the ship and load it up again with fish and shrimp for the European market.

The next day I would climb to the highest point on the island – barely a big hill but a landmark and a destination in a place like Nanortalik. First, though, I took a leisurely stroll through the town's open marketplaces. *Then*, I told myself, *I'll go get some fresh fish from the supermarket*. But by the time I wound my way to the front doors it was closed. I would go yet another day surrounded by water and no fresh fish on my fire. I scratched my head. The skies overhead were perfectly blue, only a few puffy white clouds floating across the heavens. This, however, I now knew all too well, could change in a matter of minutes. So I hurried off for the island's modest summit and a view of this place of polar bears.

Even from a low altitude the view of the surroundings was stunning. In the distance I could see a range of monstrous peaks, including the kingly mountain of granite known as Ketil. The continental ice was visible on the horizon; the fjords lay like rough-cut ribbons, sewn with icebergs swimming silently in the dark fabric. And stretching out in every direction was the tranquil endlessness of this amazing country. It was enough to forget about the fish that still wasn't in my belly. I sat on a rock and breathed deep, opening my senses to the world around me, wishing I could stay another few days if not forever.

But out of nowhere a fog rolled in, swallowing up the land until I could barely see the ground at my feet. I wasn't exactly out in no-man's land; town was a mere three kilometers away. Still, keeping a clear head in moments like this can save your day – and in the extreme, the rest of your days. Even if there is a trail at your feet, if you can't see where it is taking you it is only so useful. What few paths there are start to resemble each other after a while, and none of them have names let alone signs. You alone are responsible for knowing where you are and how you got there. Let your mind drift and you may end up wandering the land for much longer than you intended.

I thought I knew the way; I'd been wrong in this before. Suddenly this little hill was a mountain with three peaks and a dozen wrong directions. I breathed in deep and crossed my heart and put one boot in front of the other. My first steps, I could be sure, would take me in the general right direction; it was what my last steps were going to bring me to that had me worried. Though by the time I reached the foot of the tiny mountain the fog was already dissipating, and I saw to my relief my boots did indeed know where they were going.

I watched a small gathering of people as they picked wild blueberries; how easily and slowly they moved. I spotted some edible mushrooms, but this time I passed. I was feeling restless. Energetic. Light. I headed back down the short road toward Old Nanortalik.

With clear skies dominating the day once again I caught sight of an exceptional rainbow in the distance, accompanied below by a loose procession of icebergs reflecting the soft sun. I stopped, watching them barely move, soaking up another of countless moments of bone-melting beauty when I spotted a large gray object breaching the water. *A minke whale!* My second of the trip. And no French folk around to crowd my view. But the sound of a car pulling up next to me turned me around.

The father (I assumed) got out and walked around the front of the car and up to me. Mother and child stayed in their seats. *'Is that a minke whale?'* he asked. 'Yes, I think so,' I replied, wondering why the locals were asking me the questions. Then he asked where I was from. *'Oh, I know about Slovenia,'* he said. *'Your best footballer plays for Valencia.'* I listened in amusement as he went on to describe how Zlatko Zahovic blew a golden scoring opportunity in the final of the Champions

League. *Incredible*, I thought. All the way out here Slovenia has made her modest mark. Our conversation ended with my friend wondering aloud whether that whale out there wasn't actually two.

I told him I wasn't sure.

My last meal in town was going to be fresh fish or nothing. For a few minutes I soaked up the glorious morning sunshine from the ground in front of my tent; then I hustled down to the market, ready for anything with fins. On to the supermarket, where I put my fish on a shelf at the entrance like people would put their bags in a locker before entering a store back home. On my way back toward camp I saw that the outdoor fish market was still open. Figures. I also dropped in on Niels one last time, for a chat over an always-welcome cup of coffee. I bought a black Nanortalik sweatshirt, shook hands once more with my friend and made my eager way back to my tent where I cooked up and chowed down the tastiest, softest fish I've ever had the pleasure of devouring. After licking my fingers of every last bit of flavor, I broke down my tent, packed up and turned my boots toward the heliport.

Nanortalik boasts a sort of Beverly Hills part of town, where well-to-do folks live in large prefabricated houses. Beyond this neighborhood was the heliport which, on this day, was crawling like an antheap. *We'll never get off the ground,* I said to myself, half amused, half not. This was going to be my first time in a helicopter. If we did manage to lift off, I wondered if it might be my last. As it turned out, only about a dozen people were actually boarding; the rest of the crowd were relatives seeing their loved ones off.

As helicopters are much slower than airplanes and fly much lower, the flight can be exceptionally picturesque. The rotor spinning and screaming above our heads added a bit of a shake to the trip, but our time in the air would turn out to be a most awe-inspiring experience. For the entire one-hour flight we passed over fjords, mountains, lakes and glaciers too magical for words. Photographs and memories piled up, especially when we flew over Igaliku.

Back in Narsarsuaq there was time for one more hike out to Kuussup Glacier. Walking the Valley of Flowers brought back fond memories of my first hours in Greenland, when I hadn't the slightest clue what I was in for. Munching on a modest handful of blueberries, I climbed a very steep slope to a plateau dotted with small lakes. The land in front of me rose ever so slightly, running off into the sky as if it were the very edge of the world. I walked ahead, wondering if I had taken a wrong turn somewhere when suddenly, beyond the edge of the plateau, an incredible panorama of the glacier appeared. The sun hung low in the sky, throwing long shadows which I could actually see rolling over the angles and curves of the ice. It was only luck and perhaps a blessing by the Inuit deities that kept me on my feet as I scrambled like a frightened marmot one final time over the rocks and moss and lichens in front of me.

And there I stood, at the edge of the world.

I moved slowly under the extended glow of the evening sun. I looked closer at the sublime arctic beauty all around me – the yellow lichens, the scattered stones, the mowed-over meadows. Two weeks behind me, the sun shining down twenty hours a day. Now just three days left. Not nearly enough time when you feel you can walk the towns and the fields of this island forever.

THE LAND OF ERIK THE RED

My day began with an easy stroll and slowed down from there. In a land like Greenland, and a town like Narsarsuaq, hurrying will only take away from the moment. Still, I only intended to be a brief minute when I stopped in at the tourist office. Yet I found myself falling into an Arctic-paced chat with the clerk. I didn't particularly mind, but I had an amazingly difficult time trying to stick the point of my visit into the conversation: I wanted to go to Qassiarsuk, and with no ferry running (for no reason I could ascertain) I was looking for an alternative way over. The clerk rubbed his neck and rang up a few hunters he knew, but no one was heading over that day. I massaged my own neck. The clerk shrugged. *'I can take you over myself, if you can wait until three...'*

I left some deadweight luggage behind the counter and ambled off on an extremely long and lazy walk around the village. When three o'clock finally rolled around I met back up with my pack and my boatman and we walked together down to the pier. This is when I discovered my ride would be more than a simple business proposition. Several members of the clerk's family had also shown up, my transportation for the afternoon doubling as a leisurely outing for themselves. We all smiled and nodded at each other and got underway.

While Greenlanders putter around in modern outboards, they still maintain an appreciable connection with nature. As the clerk (I regret to this day not asking him his name), half his family and I motored across the fjord, the wind lifted my cap right off my head and tossed it into the water. I didn't think I'd see it again and was prepared not to care, but a guy in a nearby boat sped over, plied a tight arc through our wake and fished my hat out with a long wooden pole; a favor for me or for the water I still don't know for sure. Both, perhaps. Either way, it was another brief glimpse into the demure Greenlandic soul.

My feet safely on the shores of Qassiarsuk, I waved and thanked my nameless clerk and everyone else for the ride. Then I wandered over to the statue of Erik the Red, to try to learn a little more about this man and, perhaps in doing so, feel a little more closely connected to the land I was walking upon.

Erik the Red was born around the year 950 to a proud, strong man named Thorvald. Raised as Erik Thorvaldsson, by virtue of his wavy red hair and his exceptional temper he came to be known by his more colorful moniker. His family lived in the south of Norway; his father was a rough and violent man. Growing up, Erik watched his father closely and imitated his every move. Erik's father was quite despised for his unruly nature, but it was through his father that Erik made the acquaintance of Thjodhild Jorundardottir, a beautiful young woman from a well-off aristocratic family.

She gave birth to Erik's first son around 970; they named him Leif. Approximately seven years later, on account of a handful of murders he'd committed Thorvald was exiled from Norway. His family left with him, settling in the northwest of Iceland in a town called Drangar, in an area known as Strandir. It was here Thorvald died. Erik moved his family southward to Haukadalur and built a farm, but soon became embroiled in conflict with his neighbors. After killing two men he was forced to leave his farm and he moved his family to a small island in Breidafjord. And once again Erik fell into fighting with the settlers around him and more lives were lost.

He was outlawed from Iceland for three years, whereupon he began to prepare for quick departure. But where could he go? Not back to Norway. So he decided to go west, to seek out Gunnbjarnasker, the country Gunnbjörn claimed to have discovered but had not bothered to set foot on. Erik said he would settle the land if he found conditions suitable.

In 982 Erik the Red set sail with his family and a few friends toward this little-known world to the west. It is assumed perhaps that they approached the mainland in what is now known as the Ammassalik area and headed southwest, navigating the bergs and floes, the unusual whirlpools and the unruly Arctic temperament as they skirted the coast and rounded Cape Farewell.

That first year, when the sun all but disappeared from the sky in the coldest months, they lived in the middle of the afterward-appointed Eastern settlement, on an island that Erik would name after himself. In the Spring they sailed into Erik's Fjord, exploring the numerous connecting fjords of southwest Greenland on into the summer. They stayed in this area, surviving two more winters before returning to Iceland. Although the country was mostly covered in ice, Erik gave this land the warm name of Greenland, praising the beautiful vastness he had discovered in the apparent hopes that more people would be enticed to go settle this uncharted, untested land.

In the summer of 986 Erik guided a fleet of twenty-five ships from Breidafjord and Borgarfjord toward the new land and life waiting in Erik's Fjord. Only fourteen of these ever reached the shores of the promised green paradise. Some ships were destroyed by ice or sunken in the storms that raged around Cape Farewell. Others simply turned back. Erik the Red settled next to the foot of a mountain along Erik's fjord and made his home in Brattahlid.

Despite the rough going early on, these new settlements in Greenland took hold and soon began to prosper. Erik and Thjodhild had two more boys, Torvald and Thorstein, and then a girl they named Freydis. Erik also bore a son with another woman, contributing to his already-deteriorating relationship with his wife, bringing a sadness to his heart and taking away his ability to be an effective leader. The people he had brought to this new land felt the pain of losing their ruler, but to Erik's amazement they carried on in their wilderness, alone, with few cattle and precious little wood, whale bones, stones and turf.

Erik's oldest son Leif left in 999 for Norway, where he became interested in Christianity. The Norwegian king Olaf Tryggvason asked him to convert to Christianity all Vikings living in Greenland. He returned to Greenland the next year along with a priest who would spread the word of Christ throughout this new country.

Most people accepted this new religion, although Erik the Red steadfastly refused, even in the face of his wife's acceptance. The Vikings built the first Christian church in Brattahlid, naming it Thjodhild's Church as Erik's wife was seen there praying so often. In the winter of 1003 a wave of the flu devastated the settlement. Many perished, in some cases entire families. Erik the Red was among those laid to final rest.

Above the village stands a monument to Leif Eriksson, said to have discovered the North American continent around the year 1000. Torvald, Erik the Red and his son Leif could be considered one of the most influential exploring families that our planet has ever known.

I poked around the remains of Tjodhild's Church. There was a palatable energy in the air, like the ghosts of this place still had some unfinished business. I set out across the peninsula, past the quaint, silent farms of Tasiusaq – a few of which might not have been abandoned – along the shores of a curled inlet and on toward a dilapidated shepherds' hut that supposedly existed. The fog had been hanging thick all day, and by mid-afternoon it started to rain. I came upon a pack of polar foxes laying waste to a seal cadaver near the water. They looked up at me, mouths bloody and full. Slowly, I set my pack down and moved away. The foxes, I knew, could smell my food. But in the end it was apparent that they preferred fresh seal meat to dry pasta and instant coffee.

Relieved and on my way again, I stumbled upon a well-kept ruin of what was once, by all appearances, another church. At these times I tend to take several moments pacing in lines and arcs, trying to capture the scene before me in the perfect angle and light. This time, though, I simply took out my camera and snapped a picture of the ruins from the spot where I'd first noticed them. The weather, it seemed, was finally dampening my enthusiasm.

My day of trekking ended at 11pm, having found that the shepherd's hut I was hoping to find did in fact exist. It looked sturdy and wonderfully waterproof. And though it came as no surprise I still found a speckle of satisfaction that I had it all to myself. I'd been so eager to experience just once the solitary life of a shepherd in Greenland; now, in the waning hours of my time in this incredible land, I would have my chance.

To sum it all up, sleeping in a stuffy, dusty hut among the trash and unwanted weight left behind by those who had come before me was rather anti-climactic. Still, it was better than camping in the rain.

Through the next day the heavens kept pouring down, slowing my progress as I made my way toward the pass. The earth was marshy at best; my boots schlorped in the mud. From up ahead somewhere came the faint but distinct thunder of a waterfall. Slowly it appeared through the clouds and mist, this towering cascade I'd heard about. About a hundred and fifty meters high, this had to be one of the world's biggest nameless waterfalls.

I encountered a woman, about thirty years old if I had to guess. She was walking rather briskly in her deerskin boots, rain jacket hanging loose on her shoulders, no rucksack on her back. Her facial characteristics reminded me quite a bit of Tina from Copenhagen. Thanks to my keen insight, coupled with the knowledge and acuity that only comes after weeks (two) of trekking in the Arctic, I knew she herself was not out trekking. So there was just one question: *Where could she be going?* The only answer I could imagine was that she was on her way to visit someone, perhaps her mother, in a house I had passed earlier. *What fantastic love exists between mother and child,* I thought, *that a three-hour walk in the rain can not keep them apart for a day.* That or the girl desperately needed to go pick up her laundry.

For a while I walked along a wire fence, looking for a place I could slip through. I didn't have any particular reason in mind for wanting to sneak to the other side of a fence that I couldn't tell was holding something in or keeping something out. Maybe I'd come to the point where sticking to my original plan simply seemed anathema. But I hadn't yet found a hole big enough to assure I wouldn't get myself hung up and become food for a pack of Arctic scavengers when the fence and the path and the land all fell away, leaving me with a kingly view of wide, misty Sermilik Fjord. By now this was nothing I hadn't already seen. Yet I still felt like I was living this dream for the first time, all over again.

Not far from the water was a road – a rut, really – and I flirted with the idea of hitching a ride, not knowing or caring how far it might take me. But the only vehicle I saw was heading in the wrong direction, if there could be such a thing at this point.

Some of the farms along the edge of the fjord seemed to have been abandoned recently; most of them seemed in very good condition. And it occurred to me that no one, perhaps, pursues a life of agriculture in a climate colder than that of Greenland. Farmers here commonly keep over a hundred sheep, in addition to healthy herds of cattle and horses. I wondered if these animals appreciated the land as I turned and headed back across the peninsula.

Searching for a place to camp in the rain, in terms of sucking, is second only to having to set up camp in the rain. I pitched my tent a respectable distance from the monument to Erik the Red. (I didn't think he wanted to hear me moan about one night of damp discomfort.) This was it now; this was the grand finale, the last time I would experience relative repose amidst this heavenly scenery. And wouldn't you know it? The rain slowly, generously began tapering off. My boots had held off the water, though just barely. I put on dry socks and wrapped my feet in plastic bags to keep them warm and dry.

In the morning I went back to Tjodhild's Church and the remains of the Vikings' houses, for one more chance at soaking up the feeling and the spirit of life in Greenland. I came across one peculiar house which didn't fit in with the others, due to a kind of half-tunnel that seemed to lead directly under the front of the house. It wouldn't be until after I'd returned home that I'd realize that this was an Eskimo ruin. After the Vikings died out this area was re-settled by the Inuit, sometime during the 16th Century.

All those thoughts and dreams of discovering new Viking ruins, and I walk right by these centuries-old Eskimo remains...

To my amazement there was a man hanging out by the pier when I returned to the water. As if I wasn't more or less already at his mercy I negotiated a ride across the fjord and back to Narsarsuaq. As the airport slid into view the thought entered my head: *Does my flight tomorrow still exist?* Questions like this tend to arise once you've spent some time in the Arctic.

I dropped my rucksack on the hostel floor and walked to the airport, where I found everyone expecting to fly to Denmark that day would have to wait until Friday – and pile onto my flight. Like in no other airport in the world perhaps, nobody was frustrated or angry. Safety is the accepted priority, and flying in a dense fog and landing on a slick runway are not desirable risks. I stepped past all the people going nowhere and eased up to the counter, feeling somewhere between hopeful and ready for the worst.

133

'Yes Mr. Končnik, you are confirmed...'

I ambled back to the hostel, tired and relieved. But I also felt a sort of excitement – at the prospect of going home, to be sure, but also about the things I'd experienced here. I looked back on my time wandering this land, and I realized that in the course of my trek I saw my limits move. What before I only hoped I could manage, I now knew was not really so difficult. After some problems early on I had managed to pull myself together and continue on, all the way through to the end.

And really, this was all I had come here for.

Each one of us has a pole, an invisible force that spins the compass deep inside us, drawing us toward our dreams. For me, that pole lies somewhere in Greenland.

I think I found paradise, in a land where there are no marked trails and no signs pointing the way to happiness, fulfillment and whatever else we are searching for. But I also realize that paradise is here and now, not someplace always far away. It is what we need to create, and to live. Even in the harshest of conditions.

And this, perhaps, is what we are all here for.

SURVIVING STORM AND CIRCUMSTANCE

SECOND TRIP TO GREENLAND, 2002

Alone on the edge of an unknown wilderness. Destination: the other side. Bad luck on your tail. Storm clouds on the horizon. Countless possibilities. Two choices.

One of them is much more appealing.

In one sense, nothing will change if you abandon your aims. Life will go on. Just as it did before.

But what happens when you decide to face your storms? When you press forward through bad luck and circumstance? What's waiting on the other side, in a place you can't see?

Thanks to my pesky Nordic curiosities I'd soon find out.

In 2002 I guided my first group of trekkers across Iceland. In two weeks we managed to squeeze in three separate and spectacular trails, the first being *Laugavegur*, 'The Way of the Warm Springs.' The weather along this normally captivating trek was Icelandic all the way: a lot of rain, interspersed with spells of more driving rain. After a few hours of hiking we were soaked to the bones. Then the cold winds came. When the sleet began pelting our faces we were out in the middle of snot-freezing nowhere. But we trudged on for several more hours, in heavy silence, under the weight of our waterlogged backpacks. Having to cross a glacial river didn't help to ease the pain. I looked around at the faces following me. The consensus was obvious.

We've suffered enough for one god damn day.

In that moment I began to recognize the face of the naked soul of man, described by that most famous of polar expedition leaders, Ernest Shackleton. I could see right through the eyes of each of my people, right down to the bottom of their broken spirits – just as I suspected they saw mine. Yet we pushed on for another hour before finally finding a place to stop and cook up a warm meal.

Having had to squeeze every drop of resilience out of me just to keep going, I found out what I was capable of – as far as putting up with crappy weather goes. The men and women in my group discovered what fires burned in them as well. Each of them had to find within them a hard place, a piece of their souls that could stand up to whatever tried to erode their spirits. And as each of them pushed against the walls of their limits and kicked down the fences of their personal boundaries, our group became a team, a unit, braving the cold rains that fell on us every day save one. At some point we had ceased to be a collection of people out on a two-week hike. We had become a single entity, bound together and driven forward by the desire and the goals we shared – even if one of them was to just finish and get the hell out of there.

In the midst of our second trek I lost the trail. (Really, the trail lost me but there's no sense in placing blame now.) On the outside I remained as if nothing had happened – I think, as my group wasn't showing any signs of wanting to kill and eat me. On the last day of our third hike we had to cover twenty-five kilometers. Again, on the surface, I remained a cold-blooded creature.

But nothing lasts forever, and in the end we conquered our trails, thanks in no small part to my group's collective fortitude. Back in Reykjavik we all dried out, and everyone shook hands, traded hugs and headed home. I stuck around Iceland for a couple more days, taking in the hot springs in the beautiful valley of Reykjadalur and pondering the dry, clear weather that tends to predominate in southeastern Greenland.

In 2001 I had walked among the famed Viking ruins of the far southern reaches of Greenland. The last remains I saw, though, were Inuit. Relics of a people who had survived in this harsh place not for five hundred years, but five thousand. Relics that rekindled the fires of my imagination, inspiring me to attempt a trek across Ammassalik, a mountainous coastal island on the edge of the Arctic Circle. I wanted to find clues to the Inuit resilience, still lying, perhaps, in the abandoned evidence of their summertime encampments. I wanted to sit on the shores where men sat so long ago, watching the tides, gazing at the horizon, taking in the beauty of the world from a desolate spit of land.

Rejuvenated in Reykjadalur I jumped a prop plane for the east coast of Greenland, where her beauty would be exposed in the most gracious weather – or so I hoped after a whitewashed introduction the year before. As our plane approached the land a belt of pack ice materialized, running along the fjord-laced seaboard and off to the southern horizon. We drifted downward; the cuts and contours of the ice stared back up at us with a mix of beauty and anger. The sea turned from ripply to choppy; cracked and broken details of the rocky land appeared. Soon the water looked close enough to reach out and touch, and I thought I saw the dark shape of something moving just beneath the surface.

In the blink of an eye it all disappeared, replaced by the blur of the gravel runway of the Kulusuk Airport.

No one would meet me upon arrival today. No Tina, no Judu, not even a Jörg. From the get-go I would be on my own, which is how I wanted it to be.

Easy to say when things are going well.

From the modest, relatively smoke-free terminal I strolled southward, to a deserted lake about a kilometer out of town. I dropped my pack and gazed around.

Welcome back to paradise.

The name Kulusuk means 'chest of a black guillemot,' a reference to one of the island's peaks which resembles, they say, the chest of a black guillemot. I looked around; I had no idea what the chest of a black guillemot, or any color guillemot, was supposed to look like. Though this took nothing away from my ability to enjoy the view.

Mountains of cracked, knobby rock surrounded the lake on three sides, their intersecting slopes graced by a single glacier, snaking down and licking the shore. To the north, icebergs baring a thousand frozen teeth floated silently on the fjord's blue-black surface. *Not bad for my first night*, despite the nearby jeep tracks running up to the airport's old radar station, out of service now except as a second-rate tourist attraction.

My first impulse was to simply walk off into the wild heart of this island. It wouldn't require much planning or thought. Kulusuk appeared to be many things; sprawling was not one of them. This was probably one of the few places in Greenland where you could wander off with neither plan nor map and not put your life in danger in the process. This was a chance to feel truly free, to walk in God's garden without a thought or a care. To forget my head and follow my heart, even if only for a while.

Once I took care of my stomach.

I built a rough circle of stones to keep the wind away from my stove. My belly was grumbling, and no silly breezes were going to keep me from shutting him up.

But a malfunctioning burner might.

Are you kidding me? It was working just fine in Iceland... where I could have gotten it fixed...or gotten a new one...

I tweaked and coaxed its jointed parts. I tried hitting it with a stick. This did nothing except make the fuel slosh around in its tank. The sound reminded me of a drunken man's laugh. I didn't see anything funny about uncooked pasta for dinner.

My interest in Eskimo ruins was going south fast.

I thought back to my first trip to Greenland. I used my stove the entire trip save for that one small fire of consolation after my Blair Witch hike. This was the first time I'd have to scrounge for a real fire's worth of wood, and it was only now I realized I had no idea whether I'd be able to find any. Was there such a thing as driftwood in Greenland? There certainly weren't a whole lot of trees. In fact, there can be found precious few on the entire island, in the interior of the fjords. And they'd never be mistaken for Sequoias. On Kulusuk there were exactly no trees.

Thanks to dumb luck I found some burnable debris, in the scraps of someone else's abandoned campfire (though they didn't think to leave me any kindling, thoughtless scabs). And along the trail to the radar station I came across a broken pallet, second cousin to an old gate. Where do these things come from?

First catastrophe averted, feeling like a seasoned survivor, I jumped into my first experiment of the trip: transforming an old pallet into firewood using only my Swiss army knife. Not surprisingly, the first thing I cut was my finger. But I bandaged it up and kept sawing and slicing away until I had a pile of splinters fit for a fire.

I looked around for an abandoned can of gasoline to really get it going.

My wandering après-dinner walk brought me to the southwest part of the island. From a ridge along the hills I saw pack ice and bergs riding the current through Denmark Strait and into the wider waters of the North Atlantic. By the middle of August the arctic foliage had already turned into an amazing quilt of autumn colors – yet the flowers were still blooming. And the blueberries that were not yet ripe in Iceland were at their juicy peak here in Greenland. The late-setting sun painted the landscape in soft, shadowy greens, and for the moment my recent trial by campfire ceased to exist.

But as I walked on under dimming skies I began wondering how I was going to be able to move forward. My main ambition on this trek was to cross Ammassalik Island north to south by way of a pass with no name, passing lakes mapped only with numbers. Perhaps wishful, perhaps just foolhardy, I figured on being able to find someone in Kulusuk who could take me by boat around Ammassalik Island and up to the village of Tiniteqilaq where I would begin my trek. But the path through those steep, serrated mountains would take me up above 800 meters, and if I got hung up in bad weather, or lost my way, or ended up walking into any impassable walls of rock, I knew I wouldn't find any firewood at that elevation. No gates or pallets. And certainly no blueberries, or even mushrooms. If all went well I'd make it across the island in two quick days and I'd be on my way home. But going home wasn't the point. Neither, though, was unnecessarily putting myself at risk, which was what I'd be doing if I followed through with my original plans.

Thanks to one moody stove.

I lay awake that night, staring up at the stars beyond the nylon of my tent. Something so small, wreaking havoc with my hopes. Despondence followed anger followed determination; I wasn't going to be able to make my intended trek, but I was far from finished with Greenland. One way or another, she was going to help me see these next few days through – if only by offering me every last twig, branch and stick of hers.

I could have tried to subsist on raw pasta and snowmelt. But I wanted to live this place, not just survive it. I also had the option of retreating to the consolations of the hostel and the safety of a few day-hikes, a maddeningly attractive alternative to any surprises waiting out there on the wide empty scapes of Ammassalik (which would include, I later found out, a few polar bears). But I hadn't come all this way to seek out alternate versions of the creature comforts I'd left behind. This was an opportunity, a chance to make magic in an unfortunate set of circumstances, even if only for a short while.

All things end. I want to live before it's over.

To Ammassalik Island

By morning I was ready and pretty darn eager to face whatever was lying in wait for me beyond Kulusuk. But I hadn't even reached town when I stumbled upon a cemetery, several graves dug and waiting to be used.

Welcome back indeed.

In Greenland, and perhaps the rest of the Arctic, graves are dug during the summer, ahead of the inevitable winter deaths and the frozen, intractable ground. If more people die during the winter than there are graves prepared, bodies are stored until the thaw. Greenlanders are typically short of stature, and as I walked on I told myself I wouldn't fit in any of their graves and thus had no choice but to survive.

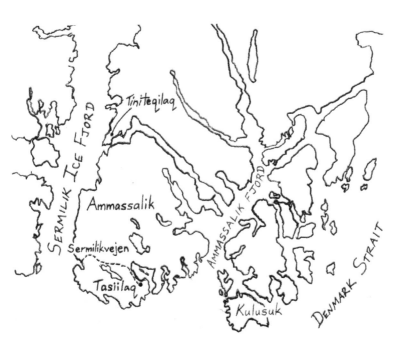

Beyond the burial grounds I came upon a row of houses, decorated in front with sleds and sleeping huskies. These led me straight to the streets of town and the Kulusuk tourist office, where I would (I thought) find out about a ferry to Tasiilaq, a village in a sheltered bay over on the near side of Ammassalik Island. But to my disappointment and surprise there were no boats heading that way.

And you call Tasiilaq the capital of eastern Greenland?

A half dozen or so hunters were shuffling about the docks, fetching ropes and lines and nets and weapons and loading up their boats. None I spoke to (haltingly) were on their way to Tasiilaq. One of them knew enough English to ask me if I had any hashish on me. I patted my pockets and held out my empty hands.

A tap on my shoulder spun me around. The tourist info guy was standing there, looking not at all surprised to find me still hanging around. Next to him stood a rather unimposing man he introduced as James. *'I go to Ikateq,'* he said, but offered to take me to Tasiilaq anyway, though not until the afternoon. *'People don't hurry in Greenland'* was his explanation. James went on to say he lived in Nuuk and was visiting his brother.

And with that he walked off.

With some time on my hands – how much I wasn't sure – I went off to find an ATM. But the only cash machine I could find, at the post office as I suspected, was out of order. The food market would accept a credit card; James, however, would not. I looked around. *People don't hurry in Greenland.* Fine then; I'd figure it out later.

I wandered off to discover the nooks and coves of Kulusuk – and found myself back at the harbor after just a few hours.

There was that day in Kulusuk a tour group from my home country of Slovenia. They were just getting back to the docks after a day-trip to nearby Apusiaajik Glacier (so I assumed from the excessively-displayed pamphlets in the tourist office). They were all smiles and laughs as they filed off their boat. My plans, conversely, were already in the toilet. Where else had they been? What had they seen? Where were they going next? Did anyone have any Kroner they didn't need?

I hung around the water's edge as they spent a full hour saying good-bye to their new Greenlandic friends. They still weren't done by the time James appeared, drifting up in his outboard with his brother.

James, boatman and hunter, was wearing thick glasses with a crack across one of the lenses. As I climbed aboard I could only hope that his other senses were a little sharper. We puttered out of the harbor and headed straight into a sea awash in pack ice, and James replaced his thick lenses with dark sunglasses. *'The sun off the water can damage your eyes,'* he explained as he wound through the mess of frozen boat killers, some of them God-blessed massive. The biggest of them had to be ten meters top to bottom, though they rose just a meter and a half above the water. These huge canoe murderers float down from the north, using the currents to bring them along the eastern coastline. The smaller floes, on the other hand, form with the freezing of more local waters.

The sea itself was notably calm, mirroring those insolent icebergs beautifully. The Greenlandic heavens above were as pure a blue as I had seen them. But this meant nothing to the mercury. We had to stop more than once on our way to Tasiilaq, to bring back to our fingertips and our cheeks the blood the freezing weather was chasing away. James pulled out some warm tea and biscuits to feed our chilled systems and liven our souls. After a word of obligatory hesitation I dug in, hunching my shoulders against the frigid winds.

When I looked up again we had reached the mouth of King Oskar Bay, a kilometer-wide entrance flanked with low-lying hills. On one side stood a simple lighthouse – courtesy of the Danes I suspected. As we moved through the bay and toward the growing hints of town I spotted a small boat, appearing to be heading straight for us. I don't know why, but I chose this moment to tell James I didn't have any Danish Kroner on me. 'I can pay you in Euros or dollars if you like,' I offered, feeling not at all like a traveler trying to impose his currency on the locals but vaguely as though I was being perceived as one. *'Pay me in Tasiilaq,'* he said, soft and curt. *'After you get some Kroner.'*

By this time the other boat was right there next to ours, and a man who might have been James's friend, or relative, or a servant of the Inuit god of the hunt handed over a few bundles of whatever it was James needed to survive while bagging his prey on the lonely island of Ikateq. To my knowledge, very few people even hunt there anymore. I looked through James' dark glasses, into his eyes, and felt very fortunate to have fallen into the very capable care of him and his brother – perhaps the only two of their kind.

Tasiilaq is the biggest town in the vast eastern region of Greenland known to the locals as Tunu. 'Tunu' means backside, which made me wonder which direction the original settlers of Greenland actually came from. We docked at port, our journey ended, and I thanked James for the safe passage. Of course our time together wasn't quite finished; we had an account to settle. Which wasn't going to happen with the Tunu ATM as useful as the one in Kulusuk. *'When will you be back?'* James asked, not a hint of concern in his voice as he replaced his sunglasses. I agreed to meet up with a relative of his once I returned to Tasiilaq – the obvious solution, I suppose – and after a firm handshake I found myself alone once again. I shifted under my rucksack and walked off in search of a place to call home.

I found it two kilometers out of town – a patch of soft, dry grass near a river with a spritely waterfall. Not far from my tent a trail ran northwest to southeast. It looked well-worn; nothing like the faint tracks of Qaqortoq. Indeed I was only there a short while when this guy came hurrying along, looking like he was running some kind of adventure race. But when he noticed me sitting there his eyes brightened. He slowed his pace and strode over.

'*My cohorts are back there somewhere,*' he said, derisive smile visible through his mosquito net. In another moment two more trekkers appeared from up the path, then after them three more. I watched them, wondering what he meant exactly by cohorts.

The six of them looked like a broken army. Obviously they were together, but the impression I got was that they were each walking alone.

From a distance it would be missed; up close it was sadly clear. This was not a group. This was a collection of individuals, staring up at the blue sky and down at the dry ground. The atmosphere was the polar opposite from that of our cold, wet trek in Iceland.

I looked at their faces. There was no communication, only disconnection. From my own experience as a guide in the

Arctic, along with my personal travels in the North, I have learned in increments the art of walking through this part of the world. Here everything is different; here guiding a group means leading people along the edge. The edge between predictability and the unknown. The edge of human experience and limitation. Of reason and irrationality. From those who choose to trek in the Arctic, a certain amount of fortitude is required, an ability to continually adjust to changing and often deeply demanding circumstances. When the members of the group can not dig these out of themselves, the guide must do what it takes to elicit them. A guide needs to possess the authority and the ability to drive the group forward – to be the first among equals. Such principles, I later realized, apply far beyond a trek in the Arctic.

SERMILIKVEJEN

Maybe this has happened to you. You're sleeping, probably at about the time you are supposed to be getting up, and a noise of some kind – the song on your clock radio, the garbage men outside – penetrates your consciousness. You don't wake up, but the noise is coming through in your brain which, by one of the great mysteries of life, takes this music or banging metal and turns it into a dream. But what's particularly interesting is, this noise makes sense as part of the dream. I remember once I listened to an entire Bonnie Raitt song while hanging out watching a grassy hillside go up in flames.

In my experience, sound isn't the only stimulus that can

infiltrate your dreams. Smell can be a catalyst for some rather odd images. I've never had a dream based on taste, for which I am supremely grateful. Sight as a dream-inducer doesn't make sense, of course. Touch, on the other hand, is a brunt and powerful beast. Specifically, the feeling that the underside of your body is being freeze-dried.

I woke up just before the evil Ice Master blasted Batman (me) in the face with his deep freeze Tommy gun.

I'm not sure how I did it but my entire body went airborne. The sound of the Ice Master's laugh was still fading as I landed in a recoiling heap on my thermarest.

My breath was thick and milky; I could just make out the ice crystals that had formed on the outside of my tent. With my body heat (and the absence of the Ice Master) the inside of my tent was almost at refrigerator level. Outside the air had to be five below freezing. But despite the chill, or because of it, the day was dawning beautifully. There was no deep-freeze Tommy gun in my face. The Ice Man had vanished. And ahead of me lay one of the most magnificent day-hikes in the Arctic.

The path winding west, across the island to the Sermilik Ice Fjord (not to be confused with the Sermilik near Qaqortoq), had the simplest of monikers: Sermilikvejen, 'The Way to the Ice Fjord.' This was the route I would follow today. I was, I'll admit, a bit disappointed at the outset; I should have been up on the north end of the island, setting out on a trek over the mountains. This of course assuming I would have found a boat going up to Tiniteqilaq, far from a given when there isn't even a ferry serving the so-called regional capital. But circumstance will have her way, and I kept my head up as I set off up a trail I would soon rename the 'Six Lakes Trek.'

The first lake, less than an hour's walk from camp, was a subtle performance of light and refraction. Closer in along the shore the water was crystal clear; a little further out the surface shimmered a deep turquoise before turning a dark, royal blue near the middle. I rolled my gaze up and back, pondering this mysterious combination of color. Maybe the morning sun had only warmed the shallow waters, producing different reflective qualities on the surface. Maybe deeper waters absorbed more light. Or maybe I needed a marine physicist to manage a clue.

Up the trail, not far from the edge of the lake, stood a dwarf of a wooden home. In the window I caught the resident dwarf staring out at me. For the next ten minutes I watched the sun's light dance on the water while trying to keep the little voyeur in the corner of my eye. When I resumed walking his face disappeared from the window. Seconds later he emerged from his house and began heading straight for me. He was typical Inuit, short with black hair and dark eyes. His clothes were a bit soiled and unkempt, but I decided to cut him a little slack for living out there in no-man's land. 'Good morning,' I said as he approached.

He walked right by like I was not even there.

No matter; the land was spectacularly welcoming. And she was much more nicely dressed than my offish little friend. Beyond this first lake stood Granite Mountain, an otherwise dull gray tinted brown and adorned with a high waterfall. The trail rose with the sloping land; the vegetation thinned. Moss grew in patches along thin crooked streams and nowhere else. I neared the waterfall, maybe 'Split Splat Fall' or something like that if it even had a name. Climbing steadily higher, my boots began sinking into the soft summer ground. I was muddy to the ankles by the time I came upon a glacier lolling in my way.

There were no cracks visible anywhere along the surface, which I thought was quite unusual. Glacial ice is not normally so slick and compact. I couldn't even get the mud on my soles to wipe off, couldn't so much as leave a smear no matter how frantically I swiped and kicked at the ice. Of course the point here was not having clean boots, or exacting punishment on the frozen monster that had decided to get in my way. The idea was that if I couldn't get a simple clump of mud to stick, how did that bode for a ninety kilogram person with muddy boots trying to keep himself and his thirty-odd kilo rucksack from slipping down into oblivion?

On the far side of this five hundred meter swath of peril I could see the continuation of the trail, slightly below where I stood. *Straight across,* I told myself, no desire to give this overgrown popsicle of death any help delivering my soul to the underworld beneath the bottom of the lake down there.

I mounted the beast on all fours and began inching along sideways.

I was halfway home when I saw the scratchy evidence of someone who had come this way before me. I found slight comfort in the fact that none of these scratch marks led downward in long, desperate lines. I clawed and toed and pled with the ice, trying not to look beyond my still-muddy boots.

After a short forever and one absolutely terrifying moment involving gravity and my fingernails I slid back onto the soft, beautifully mucky ground.

The terrain rose again, leading me up to the crest of a hill. From here I saw my next lake, this one an even deeper green. On a hillside up ahead sat two red shanties. These diminutive cottages, which can be used by both hunters and travellers, are big enough for four if the occupants don't mind squeezing together – which is probably not a wholly unappealing concept if you and your buddies are out here during the frigid winter nights. Better to plan ahead and bring an extra blanket though.

The land was still, not another human being anywhere. Just empty silence. Tranquility. Vast, barren beauty. A cold, cold paradise island, four-fifths covered with ice. My feet moved willingly, lightly forward. I peeked into each of the cottages; in one there was some leftover dried food. Not the tastiest cuisine by any stretch of the imagination but good enough to give a man the energy he needs, even out here during the sub-freezing arctic winter.

Much sooner than I expected (as if I still had any business having expectations) I came upon my fourth lake, this one a lot larger than others. Away from the water I spotted a snow partridge hunkered in her nest on the ground, following my footsteps as she watched over her cheepers. I counted about ten of them wiggling about under their mother's feathers. They were a spotty gray, making them difficult prey for the stealthy Arctic fox. (Mom seems a bit of a giveaway though.)

All along the Sermilikvejen the lakes remained on my left,

beyond them a range of mountains as high as six hundred meters. Over my right shoulder towered even higher peaks, rising close to a kilometer above the surrounding fjords. Their slopes were lightly decorated with waterfalls, white threads of water cascading fifty, a hundred, two hundred meters straight down. Vegetation was sparse at this elevation; small swaths of moss and lichens broke the brown monotony with splashes of white and light green. Boulders and rock formations appeared here and there, testifying to the irresistable forces still shaping this land.

As I approached a high point near the end of the path the Sermilik rolled into view. Mountains of earth and rock reached for the heavens; in the fjord at their feet, massive white and pale blue icebergs brooded among the million smaller chunks and floes creeping in from wider waters. Whatever whims of nature were at play here, this 'Ice Fjord' had certainly earned its name. As I took in the silent moment I thought about my earlier unfortunate turn of events.

So I hadn't been able to make my north-south crossing of the island. Such is life in the Far North, and anywhere else on this planet. That trek certainly would have come with its own moments of pure magic; yet if all had gone as planned I would never have witnessed the timeless performance of the Sermilik unfolding before me now. This was a place of such beauty that, as naturalist John Muir once put it, 'bankrupts the vocabulary.' This was a moment you could forget where you were – because it doesn't really matter. The simple wonder of the view before you becomes all, with the rest of the world disappearing in inconsequence. I might have stayed until the curtain of night fell if not for the whispering voice of reality.

My tent was still back at the other end of the trail.

Late afternoon, around five o'clock, I came upon a pair of Canadians who were just finishing pitching their own tent. I told them about the two red cabins I'd seen on the way out and just passed again. The two men looked around and smiled and said they weren't interested in moving now that they were settled in. *Fair enough,* I thought, until I noticed that they had set their tent on a ridge, in full view of the land and completely exposed to the elements. Barring an acute case of delirium brought on by, say, getting lost in Greenland, I would never have done this; I always look for a place which affords at least a little bit of natural protection against the ever-present potential of wind and rain. But one man's delirium is another man's adventure, and I smiled and wished them well and walked on.

By the time I got back to camp I had trekked a full twenty kilometers. And I still had to scrounge up firewood and cook. As I dragged myself to task a couple of children appeared, observing me with a palpable curiosity. I kept going about my work, but I couldn't ignore them when they started giggling and peeling off their clothes, obviously, deliberately trying to ruin my dinner. All but naked, they turned and ran and jumped into the icy cold bay. They whooped and hollered, partly in fun and partly, I have to believe, in sheer madness. They splashed around in the freezing water as my noodles went soft in the boiling water on my fire.

Insane as they obviously were it was a treat having them there. When they finally pulled their skinny blue bodies out of the water I waved them over and offered them part of my latest batch of pasta con carbon flakes. Their smiles could scarcely have been wider as they wolfed down every noodle I put within reach of their gray bloodless fingers. They would have sent me to bed hungry if I had let them.

TASIILAQ, AND HOME

Day Four – and already time to head back to Tasiilaq. First stop would be the harbor and the ticket office for the ferry back to Kulusuk. My master plan was to put a little extra on my visa and get some cash in return so I could pay James. The woman in the window looked at my credit card and politely shook her head. Turning away, so did I. With no other apparent options I headed for the post office, fingers on both hands crossed. And miracle of pagan miracles, the ATM was now back in service! I laughed out loud, relief giving way to the incongruity. Who around here can fix an ATM? And where was he two days ago?

Back at port with enough Kroner to buy my own boat, I found James's relative – that is, his cousin (or brother-in-law, or very young uncle perhaps, he didn't say) found me. I happily paid for my boat ride, he happily accepted and we shared an awkward good-bye. I then went and slapped down some cash for a ticket for the next day's ferry back to Kulusuk. Though the schedule read 10am the woman assured me the boat wouldn't be leaving until noon. One more glitch in the arctic matrix; no sense in asking questions. With nothing much to do but walk around town, I decided to pay a visit to the museum.

The Inuit in this part of Greenland had remained unknown to the Europeans until 1884. Before that, the Inuit probably thought they were the only people in the world. What a shock it must have been for both sides! – for the Inuit that there were indeed other human beings on the planet, for the Europeans that people actually lived in this outdoor freezer.

In the one hundred and twenty years that followed the Inuit have gone from complete isolation to a wired, modern society. There is a satellite dish on almost every roof. Fast food – burgers and hot dogs – is a regularity if not a staple. They have Internet; they follow fashion trends. And as I looked around I asked myself if their former life, their former selves, even existed anymore.

The answer, I am glad to know, is yes.

The roots of the Inuit culture run deep. Despite the modest creature comforts, hunters must still understand and respect nature if they are to continue catching the meat their people depend on. The people must defer to the demands of the harsh arctic weather if they are to survive. At the core they remain dependent on the land, now as down through the previous centuries. From my travels I have seen repeatedly that this is true.

The Tasiilaq Museum boasts a rather impressive display of

something called tupilaks. The tupilak, which represents a mystical, spiritual being, was originally composed of animal parts, human hair and even pieces of children's corpses. Those educated in witchcraft (and still allowed to roam the streets) collected these things in a remote, secret area, tied them together, recited their spiritual verses or demonic incantations and injected them with a transcendental life-force. A thus-equipped tupilak then was cast off into the sea, sent to kill a specified enemy. The crucial point here was that the tupilak had to possess immense power and strength; otherwise the enemy's tupilak would be victorious, the vanquished returning to the shores from which it had set off. Whether they did in fact harbor special powers or were nothing more than Inuit rag dolls may never be known, as no original tupilaks, neither victor nor vanquished, have ever been found.

When the first Europeans in eastern Greenland heard about the tupilak they were filled with curiosity, so the Inuit began carving replicas of tupilaks to show the Europeans what they looked like. These first model tupilaks were made of wood, with a belt of animal skin to add a touch of authenticity. Now they are carved from narwhal or walrus tusk or even reindeer bones.

Tupilaks are presently believed to be harmless. Some will maintain a certain danger still exists, though – for if you buy a tupilak as a souvenir, and then another and another until you have amassed a small army of them, the lot may mysteriously develop cult-like powers.

Buyer beware.

I would guess that one would find a kayak in any museum

in Greenland. And Tasiilaq was no exception. The kayak, it is asserted, spread throughout the world from its arctic origins. First conceived and constructed by the Inuit, this *qajaq* was used for hunting seal, walrus and even whale. The survival of the Inuit depended highly on the skill and inventiveness of the hunter; an unsuccessful hunt could mean starvation and death for the entire family. Thus the successful navigation of the kayak across turbulent waters, through waves and around surly, bucking ice masses was of paramount importance. In the thick of the hunt, if the kayak rolled the hunter had to very quickly right himself before the freezing water took away his agility, his muscle control and, ultimately, his breath.

The kayak was an invaluable tool, allowing the Inuit to venture into new and richer waters, bettering both the hunt and their chances of overall survival. But the basics remained: if the hunter didn't come back with a kill – or didn't come back at all – many others would quickly perish. The Inuit also developed a larger vessel, the *umiak*, which resembled a wide sealskin kayak. These boats were used by the nomadic Inuit chiefly to transport women, children and the elderly from place to place.

Outside the museum a small group of tourists (they're rather easy to pick out) had gathered down near the water. A couple of the locals were talking at them over a row of rent-a-kayaks.

Some things just don't change, no matter where you go.

With some subtle intrusion I found they were going off to a nearby cove, sheltered and teeming with ice floes. There they would hone their newly-acquired kayaking skills, explore a seldom-seen corner of Tasiilaq and, with a little luck, catch themselves some dinner. Meanwhile the villagers were filing out of the supermarket toting plastic bags bulging with food and beer.

No matter where you go...

I took a walk over to Stunk, a curiously-named carvers' workshop, and watched a couple of men skillfully grind, shape, refine and polish their tupilaks. The people of Tasiilaq produce the most valued tupilaks in Greenland, perhaps even exporting some to the western side of the island – presumably for the souvenir trade.

Back at nylon headquarters I kicked back and watched the group of kayakers tentatively ready themselves in the nearby water. One of the guides demonstrated an Eskimo roll in the frigid bay, then encouraged a couple of the others to try it for themselves. Though the Arctic had toughened my skin and my lightened my spirit, only one thought ran through my head:

Hell no...

The group paddled on and disappeared, and under early afternoon skies I set out on a hike around King Oskar Bay. The western shore curved gently, leading me along the northern edge of the yawning inlet. I turned inland to follow a chain of modest glacial lakes; after an hour and a half I came upon a gushing river, two meters wide all the way up and down. *Too far to jump*, I told myself sternly. Above me was a ten meter high waterfall; the pool at its crashing, roaring feet was perfect for an August swim...in Vinska Gora.

Around and up a hill and further up river I came upon another lake, a smaller version of the lake I'd just passed, which I now realized resembled every other lake in Greenland or so it was suddenly beginning to seem. Add to this the soft ground, slowly sucking my energy, and I decided I didn't need to see every single lake on the island.

Only later did it occur to me that I was walking along what would have been the last stretch of my original north-south trek.

I sat on the ground in front of my proud home, watching the evening roll in, wondering what to do with the remnants of the day when a young boy with a fishing rod strolled casually by. He was a normal kid by all appearances. So was his fishing pole. Yet there was something about him that made me stare. I watched him walk along the edge of the water and turn up the path I had just given up on.

Show off.

He'd just diappeared from sight when it clicked.

Until he came along I hadn't seen a single person fishing in Greenland, only fisherman loading and unloading their boats.

It seemed a bit late to be going fishing, but I could only assume the kid knew what he was doing. Some fish, I guessed, were most easily caught at night.

Around 2am I woke to a grunt and the patter of footsteps; in my first bleary-eyed impulse I reached for my Swiss army knife. I pushed my head out my tent door – and watched the boy turn and smile at me. He held up a clear plastic bag, fat with fish the length of his forearm. 'Bravo,' I said. He really did know what he was doing. He also had it in him to sit out in the cold night for however many hours it took to catch all those fish.

Back home a young boy fishing in the middle of the night would turn plenty of concerned eyes. In Greenland, however, it is the natural way of things. Boys are treated as men if they prove themselves able to hunt and fish, encouraging them to speed up their journey toward adulthood.

The boy walked off, disappearing into the night, and I sank once again into my sleeping bag. If I had known a few polar bears had been spotted in the Ammassalik area earlier that summer I would not have fallen back asleep nearly as quickly as I did. Actually, I probably wouldn't have been out there at all, to camp or to witness this kid walking around by himself in the middle of the night with a bag full of fresh, smelly fish.

My belly was full of breakfast. My rucksack was packed and ready. The ferry was already at the dock but I still had some time. And I just couldn't help myself; I had to go back to Stunk and get myself a tupilak. Because really, who knows when you might have to vanquish an enemy?

I was walking along weighing the risks of getting two when a man in a pick-up came roaring at me. *'You are Damjan?'* he shouted, head out the window. I studied his face. '...Yes.' Then he hurriedly explained that the ferry was set to leave at eleven, not twelve as the woman had told me. *'We are looking for you!'*

With people like this who needs tupilaks?

We roared down the street to the docks, him eyeing the ferry like it might suddenly disappear, me wondering if James and his brother were around, just in case.

I was on board half an hour before we finally pushed off.

I guess I'd had my fill of Greenland's scenery, as I found myself wandering down into the ship's innards. But why not? This is just as much a part of the overall travel experience (though hardly ever mentioned outside of a half-baked travel book). Stepping through a narrow doorway I discovered the boat's lounge – a cramped room with a table and a couple of chairs, one of them occupied by a large, haggard man. Piled up against every wall were mountains of corn flakes and bread and other kinds of cheap food, plus boxes of whatever clothes and such the locals had ordered via catalogue or, more likely now, the Internet. I also noticed a few bullets lying on the table. From Tasiilaq this ship supplied every other settlement in the Ammassalik area. And everywhere, it seemed safe to assume, people were determined to keep the polar bears away from their corn flakes.

For a solid hour our ship maneuvered among the ice floes, often bumping and nudging them aside. As we motored into the harbor in Kulusuk a large crowd gathered, inquisitive faces all staring intently as if this was their first ship-sighting. From port I made a beeline for the airport, fingers crossed that I'd be able to get on a flight. My ticket was for the next day, but with my inoperable stove leading to a complete meltdown in my plans, not to mention burdening every meal with the necessary chore of finding wood and getting a fire going, I was spent and just wanted to get back to Iceland.

I felt like I was hitch-hiking more than switching flights as I schmoozed the ticket agent.

'*It depends on the pilot*,' she said blankly.

I sat down, a humble sheep, hoping for the best as the good people of Kulusuk Airport passed the word around. One pilot looked over and gave me a nod.

I was on my way back to Iceland.

Bidding Ammassalik farewell felt like a dream, the sparse, wild landscape falling away as our plane climbed into the gray arctic sky. This island, this icy, rocky, mountainous green land, was beyond doubt one of the most spectacular and stunning places on the planet. The village of Kuummiit drifted past, far below, then the airport runway used by the US forces in World War II. The greatest moment was when we flew over Kaarali Glacier, its countless crevices running down to the tip of the glacier's tongue, where icebergs calve thunderously into the sea.

The plane turned slightly then, and the pack ice, the bergs, and the most beautiful island on Earth disappeared from view.

My head was empty, my limbs exhausted. I was doing myself a favor, I thought, getting back to Iceland. Upon arrival I jumped on a bus heading for Hveragerdi, then returned on foot to my favorite valley in all of Iceland: Reykjadalur, the Steam Valley. I stripped down and immersed myself in the steamy river, the perfect remedy for the aches and pains still lingering in both my body and soul.

Not everything went according to plan in Greenland. Not by a longshot. My boat ride to Tiniteqilaq and a hike through the Ammassalik mountains; discovering my ancient Inuit ruins;

my grand plan of trekking the length of an island wilderness; all of it, quickly and effectively done in by something as small as a faulty one-burner stove. But as it has been said a million times in a million ways, it's the journey, not the destination. I walked Greenland the best way I knew how. And I discovered the great, wild grace of the Sermilik.

This is the beauty of traveling in remote areas and in high latitudes. Or at any latitude for that matter. Storms move in. Circumstances take you where you never intended to go. And though you may not find what you are looking for, when it's all over, you may just realize you found something better than you could have imagined – not only out there, but also somewhere inside.

BETWEEN DREAMS AND REALITY

THIRD TRIP TO GREENLAND, 2006

Helena Dejak called me on December 23rd, 2005.

'It's certainly been a while, Damjan. How have you been?...'

I'd first come into contact with Helena, a fellow Slovenian and now a resident of Greenland, back in 2001 when I was in the midst of my correspondence with Clemens. I remembered giving this nice woman from Nonni Travel my number at some point, just in case.

But I didn't really think she'd ever call.

'Uh, good, doing good, thanks. Just trying to get ready for Christmas. Decorating the tree, you know...lights and stuff. So how are you doing?'

'I'm great,' she said, something lurking behind her words. 'So listen, I have a question for you.'

A pause for the drama.

I draped some tinsel on the tree.

'What would you say to a complimentary trip to Scoresby with us on the Explorer?'

'The Explo-' The phone slipped out of my fingers. *'Hello? Hello?'* Helena's faraway voice rose and faded as I grabbed wildly at my phone like it was a bar of soap in the shower. *'You still there...Damjan?'* Visions of standing out on the deck of the most magnificent and storied ice-breaking ship in history; looking out over the largest fjords in the world; soaking up once more the unparalleled beauty of the North; all these images were exploding in my head as I trampled the lights and decorations all over the floor trying to reign in the phone bouncing off of my hands. I fell backwards onto my couch. He landed face up in my lap.

The fantasies continued flashing thorugh my head. *Relax,* I told myself. Get an idea of what she's talking about. Ask a couple of questions. Intelligent ones. Go.

'Welluhwhatnow, Helena?...Wooork trip? *Whenumisit?'*

Thus began my introduction to the greatest Christmas present I'd ever received. I knew Santa had elves; I had no idea he had Helena.

'You know Damjan,' she continued, seemingly unfazed. 'We would love for a Slovenian like yourself to experience a trip on the Explorer and see the extreme landscape of Scoresby Sund – the deep fjords, the high cliffs, the majesty of the icebergs and floes...'

As if she needed to explain any further.

Another date with my beloved Greenland! And a new brand of adventure. No more would I be carrying my life on my back, survival weighing on my shoulders as I crossed the empty landscape alone, the only person at the end of the world. No, this would be a luxury cruise by comparison, figuratively if not literally. The Explorer, at heart a research ship, would not hold the sheer numbers of a typical cruise liner; I would be joining a small group of people who, I wanted to assume, understood the value of experiencing a place like Scoresby in an intimate and relatively unobtrusive way. This would be a look at a land few would ever get.

I tossed strands of gold tinsel around, wondering if I should tell the other passengers that I was riding for free.

Travelers, researchers and photographers along with dozens of dockworkers, deckhands and shipmates were crawling all over Reykjavik Port on the afternoon I arrived to board the most legendary ship to ever explore the Arctic and Antarctic: the Explorer. My bags hit the cement with an ambitious thud; I'd packed a fair bit heavier than usual. The staff just laughed and rolled up their sleeves.

On deck our group received a warm *Welcome aboard!* from the crew. Then thelines were unhitched, and at 6:45 we set sail, across Faxaflói Bay toward the tip of Snæfellsnes Peninsula, heading for the wide and wild North Atlantic. Our ship bobbed ever so slightly; I felt as though I was walking in a dream. We lined the railing and waved to the people watching us from the dock, how many of them simply curious bystanders I had no idea.

Our journey opened with a scene of living fascination so perfect I was sure it was somehow scripted. One monster of a shark slipped by our boat, just beneath the surface of the water. (A plankton feeder, it was quickly pointed out, not a man-eater waiting for someone to fall overboard though none of us gave up our tight grip on that railing.) We plied forward, slowly gaining speed, and a few white-nosed dolphins began jumping and diving and disappearing beneath our wake. A flock of white sea gannets circled overhead, squawking their playful farewells.

Magnificent. And our excursion had only just begun.

We crept up the Icelandic coast. The late evening sun fell away. The oncoming evening obscured the features of the land in a veil of gray. Gradually the sea itself faded and disappeared into the night. And one by one we went below deck to continue the journey in our sleep.

The 'Road' to Scoresby Sund

By morning our auspicious blue skies had turned cloudy; the winds, blowing moderate and steady, gave a sense of unease. What did the North have in store for us? There is of course only one guarantee when it comes to the weather in the Arctic.

Nothing, good or bad, is guaranteed.

But for the moment the air was a balmy twelve degrees. Iceland's rocky shores greeted us with a gray yet regal clarity.

Then we plowed into a freezing dishwater fog.

We sailed northwest, skirting the coast as it crept into view and faded again. We spotted several more dolphins, jumping and diving in groups of three or four. Flocks of black-legged kittiwake screeched overhead while short-beaked little auk, alongside their colorful cousins the Atlantic puffin, dove for food. Also circling and soaring were a modest number of fulmar, at first glance similar to gulls though they are actually members of the pelagic petrel family.

As we eased into mid-morning our Australian expedition leader Stephen brought us together and laid out our scheduled itinerary for exploring the largest fjord system in the world, Scoresby Sund. Along with our tours of sea and land there would be a series of presentations on the history and nature of the world we were entering. These would serve to liven the down time crossing the open seas as well as to fill in any unwanted gaps in our knowledge of the Arctic.

On this first morning Heidi, a naturalist from Canada, would give a pleasantly in-depth lecture on the various birds inhabiting this slice of the world. Two of the crew hauled out a box overloaded with binoculars, passing them around to those of us who didn't think to bring our own, even helping us tweak them to most effectively observe these birds in their natural, misty environment. Our second on-board ornithologist, Roger from England, then presented some insight into the lives of sea birds and their differing strategies for survival in the Arctic.

I was lucky to retain a fraction of the information passing through my head. Kind of like high school, except in this case I was trying. Observing these birds 'up close' was a fantastic introduction to this very special place; getting an intellectual glimpse of their instincts and abilities made me feel truly connected to their world. Even after I'd forgotten most of it.

Travel is only glamorous in retrospect someone once said. Trekking across Greenland, carrying and cooking my own food in the middle of cold, wet nowhere was certainly a tremendous experience, and one I will never ever forget. Still, I wasn't going to complain about the buffet lunch, served daily at half past twelve, prepared by a small army of cooks who had more than a busted gas burner and dry pasta to work with. The head chef was from Austria, Slovenia's neighbor to the north, while his main assistant was from east-lying Hungary; suffice to say this was a great combination, at least for this traveler. And a minor relief that our meals would not be so much to the typical taste of the Americans or (Lord have mercy) the Brits, who heartily outnumbered the rest of us.

Despite our introductory Austro-Hungarian feast (certainly not because of it) I began battling a nasty afternoon case of sea sickness. At home, in the midst of my excited preparations, this was not something I'd thought to plan for. Experienced ocean travelers know what their bodies can handle; many people are advised or have the forethought to pack some motion sickness medicine just in case. This trekker-turned-tourist, on the other hand, hadn't thought of it until he was already punching back his lunch.

I wobbled to the reception area, explaining that I was in a really bad way in case it wasn't obvious. The woman slipped into the back. I waited, expecting this ship, like most ships, would have a doctor or at least a little Dramamine hanging around. I was more than likely not the first person to ever get seasick on them.

'*The feeling usually doesn't last more than a day,*' she assured me as she handed me a box of pills. I threw a few down my throat; I couldn't wait to touch down on my cherished tundra firma.

By mid-afternoon, with nothing to see but the cold choppy ocean, several of us had gone below deck to squeeze in a quick snooze. But we were summarily roused by the announcement of the sighting of a dozen and a half humpback whales. *Whales, Damjan! Get your legs back up on deck!* Clambering up the narrow stairs I noticed my sea sickness had disappeared. *Forget the Dramamine, Doc, just give me some humpbacks.*

These enormous creatures return in summer to the waters around Iceland after spending the long winter in the Caribbean, of all places. Humpbacks, I decided when I heard this, were every bit as smart as minkes, maybe even smarter. As we moved through the water they kept diving and coming back to the surface, spraying water into the air and rolling their 30-ton bodies around. Some of them came within meters of the ship, leisurely breaching the surface and showing off the white undersides of their flippers. The crowd leaned into the railing along the ship's fore, pointing and shouting and snapping pictures, cheering like crazy each time one of them flipped its tail at us. What absolutely uncanny timing in all this, after being enveloped in such a thick fog for most of the morning. Amazingly, shortly after they closed out their performance we sailed once again into a curtain of gray.

Plowing a northwest line across the waters of Denmark Strait we encountered stronger winds and a restive ocean. With no more whales, I went back below deck to check in on my Dramamine stash.

Out on the water the Arctic climate can quickly begin sinking into your skin.Naturally, anyone heading to the far north for the first time wants to know: *What is the weather* really *going to be like?* The weather is reliably uncertain in the Arctic, but in summer it is usually quite mild for the latitude. It may be cold, but probably not unbearable and certainly not surprising to anyone who has made the conscious decision to venture toward the very top of the world. Face to the sun, it can actually be twenty degrees or more. But it is best to reckon on a healthy dose of clouds, whimsical winds and the occasional pelting rain. When the Explorer made its first voyage into Scoresby Sund in 2006 skies were sunny and clear for the entire twelve-day trip. Such extreme good fortune, however, is best left off one's list of expectations.

Relegated to a view of the thick fog, we settled in for a lecture by Susan, the ship's archaeologist. She recounted to us the story of the Viking explorers; how the Scandinavians, after settling Iceland, discovered Greenland and later North America. Next up was Thor the meteorologist (how perfect) who offered a more in-depth tale of the first people to see Iceland: seafarers who arrived under the midnight sun in a place which was neither land nor sea, but a world of floating ice shelves or so it first appeared. Helena and Sigg, our twin experts on Scoresby Sund, then presented us with 'The Land of Fire and Ice.' Sigg explained the genetic lineage of the Icelanders, the majority of men having a strong Norwegian heritage while the women shared an even mix of Celtic and Scandinavian blood. Helena followed this up with a photographic presentation of Iceland, using a lot of pictures I'd taken myself as she knew I'd been there several times. With some light conversation to go with our afternoon coffee and cake, the day passed by rather quickly.

Every evening at seven we would have a short meeting with our captain, Paul Heslop. On this day our gathering resembled more a Captain's Cocktail Hour. With typical British humor (so much more palatable than their cuisine) he gave a presentation about the conditions we might encounter in Scoresby Sound (as he referred to it) as well as along the eastern Greenlandic coast. My seasickness had by this time completely melted away.

With the storm cover to my porthole shut my cabin was so dark I had no idea what time it was when my eyes finally popped open. I wasn't even sure it was light out yet, though my system was telling me it was time to move. I opened my storm cover to the day – or night; fog still prevailed, but the sun had evidently climbed back up over the invisible horizon out there. I slid into my shoes; as long as I wasn't too late for morning coffee I was ready for whatever the day had in store.

Up on deck the crowd slowly grew as the coast appeared in the distance. The air was a brisk four degrees Celsius; in the fog arctic terns floated and dipped and circled our boat, perhaps guiding us to shore, perhaps hoping we'd show them the way. After another breakfast fit for an Austro-Hungarian emperor we gathered in the lecture hall for a brief introduction to Scoresby Sund, coupled with a glimpse into the origins and ways of the people living in northeast Greenland's only village: Ittoqqoortoormiit.

Just as Helena was getting warmed up someone outside started yelling. Next thing we all knew we were being herded out of the room and up on deck. There before us, looming and massive, was our first ice floe, drifting through the water some one hundred kilometers from the mouth of Scoresby Sund. We lined the railing, gawking and chatting in subdued, reverent wonder. We slipped along the vertical edge of this amazing frozen monster, our collective chatter growing more excited with each passing second – until a huge, cloudy red smear appeared. Everyone gasped and went silent. My eyes exploded. *Blood?* Holy crap, what else could it be? Double holy crap, from what? We all held our breath as we floated silently past...as did the red of our ship, subtly, magically reflected in the ice.

Wonderment, euphoria and mortal terror; what more could we want from the morning?

Back below deck Helena continued with her introduction to Ittoqqoortoormiit, but with all the nervous laughter still in the air I think she cut herself short. Personally I would have liked her to go on – I'd never been to a place with such a long and strange name and I wanted to know all about it. To console myself I went for more coffee; the non-Turkish variety was adequate I suppose, but once I'd sucked the last drops from my cup I set off in search of the suggestion box.

We finished off our morning going over the ever-important instructions on how to safely board and disembark from our zodiacs, the small rubber motorboats which would bring us from ship to shore and back. This, I am loathe to admit, would prove to be a parody of adventure. How did I ever make it to Qaqortoq in one living piece?

During lunch our intrepid Explorer pushed through an impressive off-shore ice belt. This meant the coast was not far off. So they were telling us anyway; for all any of us knew we might have gone right past Greenland and not known it the fog out there was so thick. *'Hey folks, special surprise for you today! We are making a complimentary stop somewhere in Canada!...'*

The approaching landscape appeared at first devoid of any sort of life. But as we sailed a closer line along the shore we began to see scattered colonies of little auk, inhabiting the coast as they characteristically do. Now don't get me wrong, little auk are mighty cute, but for people who have experienced dolphins and humpbacks and huge red smears on icebergs, birds will only captivate for so long. Our concordant interest was quickly waning. Then once again the Arctic displayed its uncanny sense of timing as our ecologist Michael pointed out three large dark blobs floating out in the water. We all gripped the railing and leaned forward. And watched. And waited. And looked over at Michael with polite irritation (I know I did).

'*Blue and humpback whales,*' he said finally. '*Pods of them.*' Then he smiled as we erupted in a calm riot. Our ship inched closer. Suddenly the entire railing was lined with cameras, an arsenal of cannons pointed and ready. To everyone's dismay they swam off before we got an appreciable look. But Michael colored in our experience with a question and answer session about whales, as he was a member of the International Whaling Commission. Who really knew his stuff.

Next Roger stepped up and painted a vivid picture of the Arctic in each of her seasons, offering delightful minutiae of the cycle of life in these northernmost climes. Did you realize that most arctic plants reproduce not by flowering but through a process known as budding and division? I don't have to tell you how much fuller a man I felt after knowing this.

Afterwards I caught up with Helena for a chat, mentioning in passing that the lectures were excellent – before asserting in a moment of hubris that I was already familiar with much of the content as I had read up on the Arctic quite a bit in the last six or seven years. '*Then maybe you'd like to give a talk on something?*' she asked. I quickly excused myself and went for more coffee.

By five o'clock the fog had dissipated again and we found ourselves staring at the mouth of an immense fjord – too vast to appreciate at first, really. There was nothing to see except water and sky and two faraway signs of land. But I knew we were only a few dozen nautical miles away from mystical, far-flung Ittoqqoortoormiit. I stood out on the deck, eyes toward the northern shore, waiting for the colorful houses of the village to appear. With shades of red predominating as I had read, mixed in with small splashes of blue green and yellow against the earthy backdrop, the sight was sure to be a memorable one. And a welcome change from the world of grays enveloping our journey to that point. But this moment would have to wait, superseded by the sight and sound of a renegade zodiac speeding toward our ship.

On board was Ib Lorentzen, a well-known Dane and former weather watcher from the village who would accompany us on our venture into Scoresby Sund. I'd never met someone named Ib before. I'd never even heard of such a name. But as he climbed on board it struck me that if I had to guess what an Ib looked like, this guy would be it.

After an official introduction and a lively dinner we were offered a partial viewing of Being Caribou, a film about a young couple who followed a reindeer herd on their 1500-kilometer spring migration across Canada. (Why we weren't shown the entire thing was not mentioned.) I glanced over at the coffee urns and wondered whether this cruise was making it more or less likely I would ever want to attempt something like that.

Probably not.

But then again, you never know.

BJØRNE ØER - BEAR ISLANDS

That our ship continued creeping forward into the night says a couple things about Scoresby Sund. One, this place was *big*. We couldn't afford to drop anchor for the night; we needed that time to cover the distances between the various aspects of the Sund we were to see. Which brings me to number two. This was not merely a sprawling maze of waterways and rock and ice. Scoresby, as would soon become well apparent, had a hundred faces and many more surprises in store for us.

So on we sailed along the southern coast of Scoresby Sund. The drone of the ship's engine played like a grown-up's lullaby; the seas rocked us gently to sleep. A light rain pattered the deck, adding to the peaceful atmosphere. Then a loud *boom!* as we plowed into some pack ice. I sat up on my bunk in the pitch black night, the theme from *Titanic* surfacing in my head. It occurred to me at that very moment: if something happened I wouldn't know what to do, other than throw my body into a lifeboat. Once I'd located one. In the black, black night.

Another berg and another boom rattled my storm cover. *Unavoidable*, I told myself. *Yes, and absolutely normal.* It had no bearing whatsoever on how skilled our captain was. *None. Definitely.* This along with the absence of cries of Abandon ship! was self-assurance enough at least to allow me to fall back asleep.

Now and then we would feel the ship tremor; a deep growl would echo through her belly as she bumped and scraped the smaller floes. It was one of those nights when you don't know

whether you actually got any sleep. It didn't help either that my cabin was in such acoustic proximity to the bow of the boat. Regardless, I was up before the gentle seven o'clock reveille and more than ready for some coffee by the time seven thirty crawled around. Breakfast wouldn't be served for another hour; in the interim a growing crowd watched from the deck as the Explorer crept by iceberg after humongous iceberg. 'Big guys,' as some of the Americans were calling them. Which was pretty much what I was thinking as I stared at a huge long-tailed skua, eyeing me from the stern.

There was an air of excitement as we gathered for a post-breakfast preview of our first trip onto the solid Arctic ground. This was on the surface our anticipation of the wonder and magic of experiencing Greenland with all our senses. But after three consecutive nights on the ship I think we were all ready for a little space, like a bunch of dogs stuck in the car too long.

Our first stop would be the Bjørne øer archipelago, a tight cluster of once-inhabited islands tucked along the northwest corner of the vast Hall Bredning branch of Scoresby Sund. We would be visiting the northernmost island, where we would see remains of the Thule Inuit, the last wave of ancient migrants to settle in Greenland. Although far from stumbling upon some undiscovered remains while traversing the wilderness alone, the chance to stand among the stones of history was still for me an exciting proposition.

The crew dropped anchor in deeper waters and we sped to the island on our zodiacs. The ruins were located in a natural amphitheater, further protected by a small island off the nearby eastern shore. The Thule Inuit constructed rather peculiar dwellings, literally digging themselves and their homes into the ground. These sunken houses (to which I gave the simple and effectively confusing moniker 'earthmen') were shaped rather like table tennis racquets, with long tunnels leading from the door down into the living space. This, perhaps, was one clue to how these people could survive more than five thousand long polar winters without central heating, vegetable gardens, iron cooking utensils or Turkish coffee.

Beyond the site of these ruins came another treat as a lucky few of us stumbled upon a revolution of lemmings – the correct and quite incongruous term for a group of these timid little creatures. They were skittering around, nosing the dirt and nibbling on green things, and as I stood there watching them I had to wonder: *Do these little critters really actually jump off cliffs together?* In the 1930's some trappers reported to have witnessed an explosion in the lemming population before they mysteriously, quickly and almost completely disappeared (the lemmings, not the trappers). These trappers then noticed that, after an exceptional season of Arctic fox hunting, the lemmings seemed to rapidly multiply. *Logical,* I thought. But the theory soon developed that lemmings periodically committed mass suicide.

In 1958, Disney (of all people) produced a film titled *White Wilderness,* for which lemmings were imported from one part of Canada to another in order to stage a fake mass-migration and suicide. Perhaps not knowing why the lemming population fluctuated so wildly, perhaps deciding the perceived answers were not viewer-friendly enough, the Disney crew set up a turntable and launched these creatures one after another off a cliff. This may not have been the only factor in the popularization of the mass suicide idea, but then again, Disney has always been a trusted and respectable name.

Neither Scandinavian settlers nor the native trappers and hunters of Greenland have ever reported actually seeing these lemmings performing their group death jump. For decades, scientists too have searched the northern regions for answers behind the lemmings' mysterious cycle of population explosion and near-extinction, but for now it remains Nature's secret. Perhaps someday a trekker from Slovenia will lose his way and stumble upon the truth.

Apart from these revolutionary, self-destructing rodents we spotted a snow partridge here and there, nestled in the ground, nurturing her young cheepers. These birds, generally a little bigger than chickens, feed mainly on the leaves and shoots of plants, as well as berries, seeds and insects. Snow partridges remain in the Arctic all year, so they are especially adapted to life in the cold darkness. Their legs and feet are covered with feathers, which helps to keep them from sinking in soft snow. They grow new layers of feathers several times a year, to blend in with their surroundings; thus they can be difficult to observe, even in broad daylight. In late Spring snow partridges lay up to eight eggs in their nests in the soil, another aspect of their survival. Snow partridges live not only in the Arctic, but also in the Alps. As we watched them ruffle their feathers I wondered who really had the better deal.

So went our first venture onto land. Ancient remnants of civilization, glimpses of the living wilderness and no huge red smears on the ground – we were excited to get to our next port of call.

After lunch we went ashore the innermost and westernmost of the Bjørn øer islands, which we found to be coated with deep, sticky clay. Straight away we divided into three groups - short, medium and longer distance hikers. And it was here that I felt the first of many huge waves of deep gratitude washing over me.

Because there I was, exploring paradise, not only on someone else's dime but with an appreciably small number of people in a most accommodating environment.

From your typical sight-seeing cruise liner a simple trip to land (where there are no designated landings let alone deep water docks) is destined to turn into mayhem. Dividing two hundred and fifty people with almost as many needs and wants into three basic touring groups, the logistical nightmare of shuttling everyone to shore in turns; the endeavor turns the ship into the Titanic, everyone scrambling and fighting to get on the first dingies. Even just viewing the land from the deck would mean standing around half the morning and waiting for a space along the rails to open up – or fighting the crowds when you realize they aren't going to move until you threaten to throw them overboard. Once on land, what kind of experience could you hope for, slogging through the clay, watching the feet of a hundred other stumbling tourists as they scare away all wildlife in a three-mile radius? How much staff and how many boats would be needed to get everyone to land and then back? How much time would it take, and what would that leave you? A few precious moments standing on the Arctic soil in the midst of the cattle herd.

This is how I imagined it anyway.

As with many people, this tour was beyond what my own pocket could afford. In this, my good fortune didn't escape me.

As I made my unimpeded way through the sticky, slippery clay I sent out another silent thank you to Santa Claus and Helena.

On this island we encountered precious little wildlife – nothing more than a few scattered birds. We did observe the multiple layers of clay under our feet; clay which thaws every summer and freezes again each winter. The main point to understand here was that thawed clay is quite susceptible to erosion by the sea and by pack ice. Thus the effects of unusually warm periods are clearly visible in the polar regions. And 2006, from the tale told by the clay, was the warmest year here in the last three centuries.

In the evening we headed for the royal stage of the interior of Scoresby Sund: the Nordvestfjord. Immediately it struck me that for such a beautiful, breath-taking slice of this God-blessed world no one had been able to come up with a more inspiring name. But it's easy to find. We moved forward, deeper into the fjord, the icebergs we passed looming larger and larger. They had calved off one of the most active glaciers in Greenland, the Daugaard-Jensen, which rolls like a frozen carpet down from the mountains into the far end of the fjord. I ceased to notice the biting cold wind as we slipped past this royal procession of pearl-white glacial bergs. Gazing at the slowly-changing faces of the massive ice sculptures floating all around us, I forgot, if only for a moment, that I had my camera with me. This, I will note for emphasis, had never, *ever* happened to me before.

At one point I climbed up to the ship's bridge, as I would every day, to check our exact location. And today, amid the grandeur of Daugaard-Jensen, in the waters beyond the North Cape, my GPS showed a new high: 71° 24. 8216' North by 25° 28.0274' West. This, it turned out, would be the northernmost point of our trip.

I made sure to get a picture.

Eventually, and only out of logistical necessity, we returned to wider waters, dropping anchor at Sydkap, the South Cape.

And there we slept, under uneasy skies, at the whispering mouth of Nordvestfjord, our ship a red dot in the vastness of Scoresby Sund.

SYDKAP

Thinking back on my early experiences with the Greenlandic weather, one word comes to mind.

Yougottabekiddingme.

Okay, not exactly one word, but the sentiment entered my head so frequently it just started to flow like that. And it wasn't only at those times when the fog rolled up like pea soup from Hell's kitchen, or when the rains just wouldn't ease up. The same feeling arose when the midday sun danced on the surface of a glacier or an iceberg; when those pastels appeared across the land and the sky in the clear, cooling evening; when the clouds turned the midnight sky jet black. Most of all, this was what went through my head as I witnessed the speed with which the sky and the land could switch faces.

By the time morning broke over Sydkap the weather had taken a considerable turn in our favor. The wind had died; the mercury hovered around nine degrees. The clouds had lifted and visibility was excellent. The dawn swam in glorious color, brawny mountains of blue and white ice floating between the yellow-tinted sky and the dark blue sea. And as I stood on deck, soaking it all in, the most fascinating idea hit me.

Six years before, as I was planning my first voyage to this land, I came across a picture of a mountain range known as the Stauning Alps. I told myself that someday I would see these rough-edged peaks for myself; that someday I would stand in their midst and simply gaze upon them. A photograph, I knew, could not possibly do these mountains and this land justice. There are astronomers and there are astronauts. And I knew which one I wanted to be.

Honestly, I can't say with absolute confidence that those mountains in the distance, bathing in the light of the morning sun, really were part of the Stauning range. But they were just as beautiful as I remembered the ones in that picture to be, so I decided to run with the thought. When I took my first serious look at a map of Greenland I knew that someday I would have to come walk in a world without trails – to test the limits of what I could do while seeking out some of the most beautiful places on Earth. I wanted, too, to see this place, this Scoresby Sund, where regal fjords reached into the land with wide, winding fingers, watched over by these fantastic, forbidding peaks. During my correspondence with Clemens we found we shared the dream of visiting this spectacular little corner of the world – though neither of us had any workable idea of how to actually get here. At first I suggested Clemens e-mail Nonni Travel. He wrote back saying he was in the middle of university examinations and did not have the time. So I wrote them myself – in English since I didn't speak Icelandic and I didn't think my German would get us anywhere. What a shock it was then to get a reply in Slovenian! Disappointment soon took over, though, as I had to tell this very nice woman named Helena that the journey was, for us, financially out of reach.

Five years later Helena came back and invited me on the trip of a lifetime. Which may not have happened if Clemens hadn't been so studious a guy.

Those of us going on the day's long hike were ferried ashore first, with those hiking the shorter trails to come after. Not long after setting off up the trail our group came upon a white polar rabbit, an accommodating little creature as he sat still for us while we all angled for photographs. Reminding myself where we were and what sort of climate predominated here, I found myself lending this little ball of fur a lot of respect.

On a plateau we encountered about a dozen grazing musk ox – *umimmak* in Inuit, meaning 'long-bearded one.' With both males and females sporting long, curved horns and weighing as much as four hundred kilograms, these animals are often mistaken for cousins of the buffalo. Oddly, they are more closely related to goats than to buffalo, or ox or even cattle. Their long brown and black hair almost touches the ground, a wooly coat seven times warmer than that of sheep. They inhabit a wide expanse of northeastern Greenland, and are also especially prevalent in the western Kangerlussuaq region.

As we were watching, two males began butting heads in an apparent battle for supremacy in the herd. Either that or they were fighting over whose turn it was to pose for the god-damn humans. Neither did though, and as it was the start of the mating season we decided to keep our collective distance.

During the summer these musk ox prefer to graze the river valleys, where the vegetation is thick and lush. Here they feed primarily on grass and shoreline cane-breaks. In winter they withdraw to higher altitudes, where, interestingly, there is less snow. Their metabolism slows as food becomes less abundant, but despite the harsh seasons a single herd may grow to more than three hundred males, females and juveniles. As we made a loop around the plateau we came across some of their skeletons, evidence perhaps of their greatest enemy, the Arctic wolf, still very rare in northeast Greenland after they were hunted almost to extinction in the mid-20th century.

When we returned to shore we had time to check out two spots where, a few centuries earlier, small groups of Inuit set up summertime tent residences. While in fair proximity to the tundra where they grazed their livestock, from their vantage point near the cape they would have also been able to closely observe the tides and the moods of the sea. As the winter approached they could then keep an eye out for migrating humpbacks and hitch a ride down the the Caribbean. (Well that's what I would have done.)

Along the shoreline we discovered the skeletal remains of a narwhal that had been caught and utilized by the locals. I say utilized because in the Arctic, resources are rare and therefore precious. Nothing of a catch goes unused. Except, apparently, the skeleton.

Along the hilly coast we saw more 'earthmen' excavations. Not far away were a few of the area's operating game posts. Through the 20th century a number of commercial stations were built, giving the locals a place where they could sell seal skins and other such catchings. Along the coast also runs an extensive network which supports the crucial Arctic trout fishing industry. Standing on the desolate shore, it was both easy and difficult to comprehend the necessity.

CIRCUMNAVIGATION OF MILNE LAND

In case it isn't obvious by now, Greenlandic place names can be quite long. Ridiculously long. Comically long – until you have to pronounce them. This must have been what the Danes were thinking when they renamed the fjords, islands and capes of their new land.

Back on deck after our walk among the hills and fields and ummiak shit of Sydkap, we weighed anchor and sailed south and west into a long fjord with the following name, which I am not making up: Ø.

On the north side of Ø Fjord the peaks of Renland reached for the heavens with countless sharp brown angles. Glaciers snaked down their cracked and broken slopes, winding toward the water. To the south stood the Milne Land High Mountains, their edges and peaks, in contrast to their Renland counterparts, worn smooth by time and the elements. Impressive walls of rock lined the fjord on both sides, in places rising virtually straight up out of the water. In fact, we were told, just a few weeks earlier two Norwegians had scaled these very walls, their climb starting when they literally stepped off their boat and onto the cliffs disappearing into the icy sea below their feet.

We ourselves would not be attempting anything quite so extreme, but we did have the option to go zodiac cruising. Most of us jumped at the chance to experience these fields of floating ice up close; a few, though, were content to observe the scenery from the ship's deck (and in that time gulp down the rest of the day's coffee I suspected).

From the surface of the water we could see in the distance a remarkable natural bridge of ice, carved by wind and water out of a thick wall of a berg. I was the first to speak up and ask the leader of our little rubber boat if we could try to maneuver for a closer look. As expected, he was more than happy to oblige.

Along the way we paused to check out this magnificent turquoise iceberg, slowly melting away with the gently lapping water. Then as we neared a second spectacular mass of ice we heard a deep, ominous popping sound. *No way*, I thought. But yes, this was the sound of trapped air bursting from pockets in the ice. Which, I knew, meant one thing.

A boom shattered the air as the iceberg we were heading for collapsed and crashed into the water in pieces of a thousand sizes. The sight was positively heart-stopping, for better or for worse. The sound was no less impressive. But strangely, the first reflective thought that ran through my mind was that the passengers still drinking coffee on board probably had the best view of all of this. Closer though we zodiac trippers were to the action, we were in a difficult position to see and appreciate in its massive entirety the thunderous collapse happening literally right in front of us. (We were also preoccupied with holding on and saying our prayers.) Our friends on board could probably also see, much more clearly than those of us on the water, the relative immensity of the glacial bergs all around us. And once again we were all reminded how small we really are when we immerse ourselves in a landscape and a world such as this.

As if to welcome us back from the brink of non-existence, our chefs had prepared a barbeque picnic for us up on deck, a casual party that would spill right over into dinner. On board they had hung the flags of all the countries represented by those partaking in this Arctic odyssey. One flag, however, was missing – the white, red and blue of Slovenia. Maybe I was supposed to bring my own; maybe freeloaders didn't get a flag. I didn't mind though, as long as I got a plate and a coffee cup. In the meantime the clouds had all but disappeared, revealing brilliant blue skies. The sun turned the snowy peaks and floating bergs a pure, perfect white. The water had also taken on a bluish tint.

Paradise wears many moods and colors indeed.

In the midst of filling up on roasted ham and sun-washed fjords we were treated to yet another crashing, bone-shaking performance. From a huge iceberg off our port side a stream of trapped water was spilling into the sea. Obviously this water had just made its escape; we all knew something was afoot and dutifully packed the ship's railing. Suddenly the berg growled and cracked, and a huge chunk of ice broke off and crashed into the sea. This was the second of three icebergs that would collapse right before our widened eyes, in a great and terrible demonstration of the tremendous forces of Nature.

We continued southwest, the cliffs and slopes of Milne Land curving away, leading us into Snesund, the 'Snow Sound.' Here we found our starboard flanked by the reddish-brown rocks of Stor Ø (which, by the way, I do not know how to pronounce). This triangular Big Island, a barren cluster of mountains, boasted a single serpentine river of ice, playing hide-and-seek among the rough peaks as we crept by.

Snesund brought us past the southern tip of Stor Ø and into Rodefjord, so named for its massive banks of rock striated with bands of dark orange. We turned and sailed northward, the waters of Red Fjord spread much wider than those of Snesund. On the sloping fields between the orange and gray rocks we spotted several more small herds of musk ox. Reaching the northwest corner of Stor Ø we found ourselves reentering Ø Fjord, now in its far western reaches. Across to the northeast lay the mouth of Rypefjord, the 'Snow Partridge Fjord,' where we once more dropped anchor for the evening.

Morning broke in blessed fashion – sweatshirt warm, with only a slight breeze blowing. The pagan god of the sun was smiling on us once again. But we all knew by this time how fickle and whimsical the Aesir can be, so after breakfast we set off straight away for the deepest reaches of Rypefjord.

Here the sloping tundra was a marbled mix of green and gray. As in other places, herds of musk ox roamed the pastures in the distance, perhaps oblivious, perhaps determinedly disinterested in the outsiders come to ply their private fjord.

Ahead of us the Eielson Glacier rose from the water up into the mountains, stretching out over more than a kilometer. Now think about this. We're sailing through a channel of pristine water. We're surrounded by miles of mountains, all plenty tall enough to swallow the world's tallest buildings and have plenty of room left over for dessert. In front of us is a ribbon of ice, several football fields wide and more than ten – *ten!* – football fields long. The sun is shining. The air is immaculate.

Someone please explain to me the lure of a hotel room in Waikiki...

We anchored near a valley of muted greens fronted with sandy beaches, and a group of us jumped ship for a long hike up into the hills. If you've ever hiked down into the guts of the Grand Canyon you've seen how completely different two angles of the same place can be. From below, the famously sweeping views of the Canyon cease to exist, replaced by a river gorge that holds its own charms but is not at all the same. Landing on the shores of Rypefjord brought the same sense of 'Where'd it all go?' (Okay, so this doesn't happen in Waikiki.)

The majesty of Eielson had disappeared, replaced with views of grazing lands. The ground was marshy underfoot; we discovered some fresh tracks – evidence of a herd of musk ox recently passing through. Also scattered about were strands and clumps of discarded wool; the ox were beginning to don their thick winter coats in anticipation of the long arctic winter. The climate inside the fjord system, though, is considerably warmer than along the coast. In fact, this region is considered the 'low' Arctic, despite lying at the 70th parallel, just one more sublime reminder of the many facets of this land.

We moved slowly forward, picking blueberries which were at that time perfectly ripe. The next pause in our hike came courtesy of some long-eared polar rabbits. This truly was the perfect day for someone who loves taking in both the simple beauty and the grand magnificence of the Arctic. We moved easily along, each of us gathering up bits of souvenir wool.

At times I strayed ahead of the group, in other moments I let myself fall behind, in the leisurely pursuit and pleasure of photographing the myriad aspects of this incredible world. But gradually it dawned on me that it would be worth it to step up the pace; with all the ox hair (and dung piles) we were seeing, what might we encounter up close, further up the trial?

Several times along our hike our guide paused, creating for us the experience of listening to utter silence. A couple of times we did the same at the request of one of the other hikers. But our Dutch photographer had something else in mind when he turned and put his finger to his lips. We all stopped walking. No one made a sound. He pointed at the trail up ahead.

Not far away, a huge female ox grazed the land with her tiny, stick-legged calf. After a brief moment of communal wonder we began slowly reaching for our cameras. These animals have an incredibly sharp sense of smell though, and despite our efforts to keep perfectly quiet they sensed our presence and hoofed it out of sight. For many of us this was one of the finest moments of the day, despite the nascent thoughts of the lot of us needing a good shower. Soon thereafter we encountered a third ox, and for several minutes we watched him and he watched us, neither side less curious than the other.

Further ahead we encountered half a dozen Arctic geese, floating silently on the surface of a glassy lake. The females lay their eggs on the cliffs above, it was explained to us, but once the goslings hatch the mother brings them out onto the water where they remain safe from their main predator, the polar fox. Beyond this peaceful scene a wide, shallow river tumbled down from another lake, spilling in a waterfall down into a canyon and toward a distant river delta. In this area lie part of the boundary of the largest national park in the world, the National Park of Northeast Greenland. I know that I saw the park, at least in some very small part, but I can't say for sure that I was at any time actually *in* the national park, which boasts an area forty-six times that of Slovenia. Though out here there seems little point in even bothering with boundaries.

Unlike the trip out, on the way back to our zodiacs we were confronted by some startlingly aggressive wildlife. We were doing nothing that I could tell should provoke a response, and a terribly angry one at that, from the denizens of this land. Yet out of the clear blue sky a squadron of arctic terns launched a sudden barrage of air attacks on our unsuspecting souls. First one of them dive-bombed the men leading our group; it looked like he was aiming specifically for our Dutch photographer. Before long I too found myself a target in this hectic ambush. I called them all kinds of names as I waved my arms wildly about my head; I wanted them gone, these oversized pigeons. The truth is, though, these terns are quite exceptional birds.

They are hardy world travelers, migrating tens of thousands of miles each year. They fly up from the Antarctic in Spring, nest and rear their offspring, then fly back to the Antarctic, all on a diet of insects and the occasional fish they manage to snatch from the surface of the ocean. Arctic terns are white with greyish rears and black hoods on their heads. Their legs and beaks are red. Their tails are split into long skirts. As far as birds go, they look pretty darn intimidating. We must have walked into their nesting area, as they nurse their offspring in holes and hollows in the tundra or on the stones along the shoreline. Females lay two to three eggs at a time. Their babies sport a highly protective color scheme. If anyone comes too close the parents attack with both claws and beak; and, as we were well aware by now, they don't fool around. In October, as the region grows dark, they retrace their long route back to the extreme southern reaches of the Earth.

Shortly before noon we returned to the ship. Thirty minutes later another fat buffet lunch spread was waiting for us. *Travel is only glamorous in retrospect.* That person had obviously never been to Scoresby on the Explorer.

As we filled our plates our crew weighed anchor, and we exited Rypefjord. Crossing back over Ø Fjord was like riding a sea of silk; then we dipped once more into Rodefjord and a world I swear I had never seen. The fjord seemed now to have donned a new face, mysterious and strange as another planet. The water was like glass, reflecting a darkened mirror image of the ice and the orange-striped rocks. The color and formation of the bergs and floes resembled a string of mangled pearls, sharp, bright and opaque against the dark waters. We slipped quietly along; the reflections and images and ice appeared to move right along with us. To me they seemed alive, following us with their stare, silently urging us to leave this place before it was too late. I snapped a photo, then another. The animate aura of Rodefjord, alas, was wholly absent in two dimensions.

But the ghosts of Greenland weren't done with me yet.

I stood enchanted. Enraptured. Slightly spooked. And in a quandary. Do I stay and let this stark moment sink into my memory, or do I run below deck and fetch the minicam I'd stuffed into my pack at the last second? I backed away from the railing, eyes stuck to the water and the land and the sky. Then I said a quick prayer and bolted down the steps and down the hall to my cabin.

What a beautiful thing that the voltage and frequency and outlets on board matched my equipment perfectly. My heart is in Nature; still I can't deny the beauty of technology.

I raced back up on deck.

My ghosts were nowhere to be found.

In the afternoon we took off again in our zodiacs, to get up close and personal with a few more bergs. Approaching our first monster, we noticed some incredible variations in its color. At times cracks form in the ice, and when water runs through these cracks and then freezes it results in zig-zags and spider webs of a different hue. The ice in front of us sat in barely perceptible shades of white, incongruously marbled throughout with a brilliant turquoise blue.

Now try to imagine these icebergs, layered in whites and veined in blues, floating in countless shapes and sizes. Add to the picture some arctic terns and a scattering of seals. The seals are lazing on shallow ice floes; terns are shaking out their wings and surveying their surroundings, fresh catches of small fish at their feet. You are gliding across the water toward a mountain of ice so pure it is practically transparent; only a thin veil of sapphire blue gives it color. The sun in the eternal blue sky feels warm on your face. The air is cool, ticking your cheeks, and so clean you can feel it cleansing your lungs.

This, my friends, is but one more moment, one additional glimpse into the unsung paradise known as Greenland.

We looked closer at the turquoise-laced berg before us. A sweeping patch of lighter blue testified to the recent calving off of a huge chunk of its ice. Our Dutchman angled for some underwater photos before we zodiacked on to Rode Ø, aptly named as it is predominantly composed of soft red sandstone. Along the nearby cliffs we observed a number of nesting gulls, their pups still covered with gray down. On the southern side of the island we could see thin lines of hardened magma, the sandstone around these geological blood vessels having already eroded away.

On the northwest side of Red Island we came across a large colony of terns. We moved slowly past; none of them attacked us. Back on board the ship we sailed toward the most southerly point of our trip through the inner fjords, round the southwest corner of Milne Land and through long and narrow Fon Fjord. Dry, warm winds tend to predominate in this corridor of the fjord system, but on this day the clouds had begun to move in and before long we started feeling raindrops. Bad weather is a bummer wherever you travel. In a place like Greenland though, where the sun can play shy for days or weeks at a stretch, the focus shifts. When the rain sets in you shrug your shoulders and thank the heavens for holding off for as long as they did.

If they did.

We braved the worsening weather for a while, but one by one everyone began to take shelter.

After dinner we were given a pop quiz about our knowledge of the Arctic. Sad to say, even with all the reading up I'd done, my group finished somewhere in the middle. (Thanks to my keen avoidance instincts and my earlier hubristic display with Helena I hadn't told anyone on my team how smart I was.) Late in the evening we anchored off the sparsely-vegetated north side of Danmark Ø, where the waters of Fon Fjord and Heslop Bay quietly converged to rock us gently to sleep.

For a brief moment when I woke the next morning I thought I was in Scotland. The dense cloud cover wasn't unusual, but the gray seemed a product of slightly warmer climes. The light spray off the water as well brought a strange sense of elsewhere. But Scotland doesn't quite measure up to Greenland when it comes to ice shelves blanketing the land, and soon enough all was well in my mind once again.

The peace of this place, in case I haven't belabored the point by now, is remarkable. A group of us hiked for the major part of the morning along the fringes of the relatively intimate Fon Fjord. And here again we stopped and listened (maybe for the last time) to the enveloping silence of this desolate place. A minute passed by, maybe more. We stood in utter silence, tossing playful grins around. Until a heinous chorus of shrieking birds rose up in the distance.

Memories of a recent ornithological ambush still fresh in some of our minds, we nevertheless voted to go investigate. A few minutes' walk brought us to a wide plateau where floating on yet another emerald lake were perhaps fifty Arctic geese. In Summer these birds make their home in eastern Greenland; as Winter approaches they head to the Hebrides Islands west of Scotland and Ireland. Looming above the lake was a tall, sheer cliff. This, I did remember from my casual arctic research, was the exact sort of site where every year an incredible drama unfolds.

Arctic geese build their nests on cliffs to keep their eggs and offspring out of reach of foxes and other such robber types. However, like many geese, this arctic variety does not spend a lot of time coddling its young. The new parents barely bother to fetch their squeaking goslings food. It was long thought that young geese were hidden away on the ground under rocks, but the truth is more amazing than a lot of people would believe.

At the ripe age of about three days the goslings jump from the cliffs. Not pushed out by over-expectant parents, not blown away by sudden and stiff arctic winds. They jump, of their own volition (as much as baby birds possess) from nests which can be as high as several hundred meters off the ground. Their light weight and the fact that they are covered with thick down helps some of them to survive this free fall, but many are injured, others die, and the rest of the unlucky fall immediate prey to polar foxes, in part thanks to the cries of the distraught adults as they watch their young plummet to their assorted fates. The survivors are then herded into protected nests or onto the lake, drawing the curtain on one of the most bizarre spectacles in nature and a graphic picture of the never-ending struggle for survival in the wild.

Before these arctic geese had a chance to mistake us for a pack of hungry baby bird eaters we turned and headed off, on a trail that would loop through the land before spitting us back out onto shore. Along the way we encountered a wonderful variety of nesting birds: snow bunting (sometimes referred to as 'snowflakes'), some wheatears (a name derived from the term 'white arse') and a small group of red-throated divers. We paused at the sight of two polar hares, surprisingly close to the path and seemingly unfrightened by the forest of legs slowly moving toward them. We inched closer and closer, snapping photos until they finally hopped away.

As if to remind us that she is not all cheeping birds and fluffy hares, Greenland tossed a small spit of a glacier at us as we were making our way downhill toward shore. The elderly couple with us wore a mix of resolve and trepidation as they stared at the ice at their feet. These were the folks I would expect to be on deck drinking my coffee, but here they were, out on the tundra, taking in all the green land they could before our time here was up. After giving them a moment to preserve their dignity – as if they had anything to prove – I put out my hand and helped them across.

And with this final obstacle safely traversed the gentle face of Greenland returned, in the form of a pageant of Niviarsiaq flanking the river splitting the land before us.

At the water's edge we were brought some towels, and the most courageous (read: stupid) of us stripped off our shoes and socks and rolled up our pants and waded into the ice-cold sea – which was all of four degrees we were told. The idea brought cries of agony out of all of us, including those still standing with their boots on dry ground. Our trip leader then challenged all twenty of us to stand in the water together, the incentive being he would then let us throw him in. But there were only sixteen brave (read: idiotic) souls among us. I'd say he was banking on at least the elderly couple declining.

All feet back on deck, we began plowing our meandering way toward Ittoqqoortoormiit. During lunch we sailed across the gaping mouth of Gåsefjord (Goose fjord), at the southwest reaches of Scoresby Sund. The worming fjord was teeming with bergs; we wouldn't be attempting a trip down Gåsefjord's gullet today. The clearing skies were fair compensation, affording long, slow glimpses of Cape Stevenson and the low hills of Flakkerhul, in southwestern Jameson Land. In this part of Scoresby, out closer to the open seas, the floating ice was merely the foundation of the vast and striking scenery. Behind us, the snow-covered peaks of Milne Land rose like a desolate pathway to heaven. To the south, a solemn procession of glaciers lolled silently down from the Geikie Plateau.

We received an above-deck lecture by Susan, our esteemed archaeologist, who described in vivid detail the development of Greenland, the strong Danish influence and the colonization of the capital city of Nuuk. As we listened, intent and completely unsuspecting, male lumen began darting about the air above us, in ever-increasing numbers. Before we knew it the air was filled with the rapacious arctic gulls. Where had they all come from for heaven's sake? By now we didn't know what to expect from these birds and were all kind of crouching down, each one of us looking around at the others, trying not to be the tallest target out there on the wide open deck. The dive-bombing we were all fearing never materialized though; lumen, when their young are not in danger, prefer bread crusts and saltines to human flesh and eyeballs.

Back on our feet the excitement continued as we caught a glimpse of a narwhal swimming lazily off our port side. We rushed the railing. The lumen kept screeching. Greenland was once again showing a lively, hectic face. Then just as quickly as the commotion rose up it disappeared, leaving us once again to the placid waters of the Sund.

203

We continued along, tacking smoothly across Scoresby, the abandoned village of Kap Hope appearing on the horizon.

Kap Hope was inhabited until May 2006, when the last of the persevering villagers finally up and moved, eastward to the nearby settlement of Scoresbysund, referred to by the natives as Ittoqqoortoormiit. After all the animation and wonder of the day's events and the grandeur of our surroundings, this final tidbit served as a poignant segue to the idea that our trip and our time were drawing to an end. And below the spirited surface, our conversations with Helena, Sigg and Ib took on a quiet solemnity. Such is the case when you share with others not just good times, but moments which elude explanation.

Before dinner we had a chance to sample a local specialty called mattak, made of raw whale skin and narwhal fat and, apparently, rich in vitamin C. Then some of us went on a little side trip to Kap Tobin – *'to see something special'* as Sigg put it. But somehow in the process of readying the group for this surprise excursion I got roped into carrying a load of supplies and equipment to Helena and Sigg's summer house there in Kap Tobin. *'Got some home repairs to tackle,'* Sigg told me, as if that should help make sense of everything. At least I had some help, in the form of a young sparkplug named Ludvik, while Sigg took the rest of the group on an evening trip to Unartoq, the hottest spring in all of Greenland, with ground water bubbling up at a toasty sixty-two degrees Celsius. From four-degree sea water to scalding springs; this was indeed a land of extremes. And, of course, the occasional home repair.

Finished with our grunt work, Ludvik took a look at all the debris and trash scattered around Kap Hope and decided to rename the abandoned village 'Kap Mess.' I kept silent, trying to figure out just what Helena and Sigg were up to here.

ITTOQQOORTOORMIIT

Our ship moved quietly through the gray of the early morning, nosing toward the most isolated settlement in Greenland: Ittoqqoortoormiit. It is interesting to note here that until fairly recently, Inuktitut, the native language of the Inuit, had no written form. Beginning with a group of Lutheran missionaries, who in the 1700's translated the New Testament into Inuktitut using the Roman alphabet, the language developed a healthy amount of variation across Greenland and Canada. Particularly diverse are the spellings of certain place names. This should come as no surprise in many instances though. I mean really, how could an entire town, never mind an entire culture, agree that 'Ittoqqoortoormiit' is the best way to spell something?

On a positive note, the concept of street names has yet to take hold here. Imagine the size of the envelope you'd need to address a letter to this place.

The first residents of this robustly-named small community, located on a spit of land at the mouth of Scoresby Sund, arrived on September 4th, 1925 on the passenger ship Gustav Holm. On board were approximately seventy immigrants, moving here from the over-populated Ammassalik area. On the way they detoured to Iceland, specifically Isafjord, where a bout of the flu began to spread. Eventually it became an epidemic, taking the lives of the oldest and weakest of the group.

The rest sailed on to the east coast of Greenland, battling the flu, settling in a lean, infertile, unknown land, the start of their new life looking frightfully unpromising. Yet they soon found the hunting to be much better here than in the land they'd left behind; in the first year they caught more than 1,000 seal, 115 polar bear, 71 polar fox, 70 walrus and 8 narwhal, allowing them to remain on the more forgiving edge of survival.

In contrast to the harsh life the early settlers faced, there are now year-round pleasures here for the rare traveler. In winter one can go on a dog sledding trip, or ski mountain slopes with no lifts and no names; in summer there is trekking of course, for pleasure or for research or for the sheer challenge. This applies as well to kayaking in the fjords.

Our itinerary included three hours in Ittoqqoortoormiit. At first glance this seemed ample time for such a modest endeavor. But the four hours we ended up staying for felt sadly fleeting. For the locals, who number about five hundred, a visit by a group of eighty people can constitute a fair disruption of their lives; there is good reason for the three-hour time limit. But the people of this tiny town opened their arms and their doors to us. Local doctors welcomed visits by any traveling colleagues, to sit and share their adventures with them and the residing nurse. The meteorological station people opened up their facility, offering glimpses into how they work to predict the ever-changing weather. The townsfolk invited us into the church, the museum and the tourist office (though this we might rightly expect). Before we arrived some of the local fishermen had caught a few narwhal; by the time we got there though the mattak and meat had already been sold, leaving us tourists nothing but bones. A select few in our group had the chance to go to the local school with Helena, to see the kids at work (play, actually) and meet Greta, one of the teachers and a dear friend of Helena's.

We visited the jail – apparently there is need for one – and the smallest police station in the world, complete with one police officer. In front of the building the policeman's wife was busy cleaning a narwhal tusk.

After a stop in the general store I went to the tourist office, which I heard was originally the sacristy of a church. Seems the locals decided to place their fledgling tourism industry in the hands of God. Outside I came across a group of four Germans who had just arrived in town – on foot it was quite apparent. They were carrying with them large caliber guns, which meant (I hoped) that they had just trekked across polar bear country. I stepped up to ask them about their journey – and saw four faces, four pairs of eyes, with nary a trace of emotion among them. One of them looked like he had lost his very soul and didn't even know it. From the other three as well there was barely a hint of awareness that there was some guy standing there talking to them. It reminded me just a bit of how I felt in the middle of all those kids in Qaqortoq.

Slowly I was able to drag their story out of them; these four men had just completed one of the most physically and mentally demanding treks in all of Greenland, walking for three days through polar bear country with little sleep, then more than twenty hours on the fourth and final day. *'Just getting up and moving was borderline impossible,'* one of them said.

Barely.

Listening to their words I knew they were happy, deep inside somewhere. 'My hat goes off to you guys,' I said. 'All the way to the ground.' Then I patted them on the shoulders and congratulated them on their brave trek and told them I'd never met such adventurous men. I had those moments of physical and emotional exhaustion too, during my first adventure in Greenland, when even the hairs on my arms were lying flat. And I knew how they felt at this moment, at least to a degree, as I'd experienced a similar feeling – or lack thereof – when I finally made it to Qaqortoq. I assured them that eventually they would feel the excitement of their accomplishments, rising up from that place deep inside them, a little brighter, a little stronger each day.

They seemed to want to believe me as we bid each other *Auf Wiedersehen.*

They disappeared inside the tourist office and I headed off to see the place where the local hunters kept their dogs. During the summer months, when dogs do not work, they are fed less often. They are usually given seal meat, though on this day they were being treated to narwhal steaks. And a few leftover bones, perhaps, for dessert.

BLOSSEVILLE COAST

Our time in Ittoqqoortoormiit had come to an end. Ib, Helena and Sigg bid us farewell and returned to their lives. On the quay a number of children had gathered, and they waved to us as we sped across the water on our zodiacs, back toward the Explorer. They were still waving as our big red ship turned and headed for Kap Brewster, at the southern lip of this fjord-filled world I wasn't yet ready to leave.

Back out on open waters we sailed southwest past the three rocky islands of Dunholm, site of an impressive array of bird colonies. The calm afternoon ocean allowed for a zodiac trip around the southernmost island, where birds sat scattered all over the basalt cliffs. Most adults had one or two young with them; some coddled babies still clothed in their warm gray down. We saw fulmar resting their wings here and there; we observed black guillemots nesting in the cracks and holes in the rocky cliffs, constantly catching and bringing in small fish for their always-hungry offspring. I tried, but I just couldn't see the resemblance to any of those mountains on Kulusuk.

Continuing around brought us to a small, densely populated colony of kittiwakes and their perpetual chorus of heinous cries. Not far from this we spotted a cousin species of the kittiwake, decked out in slightly varying colors. Observing these birds it was interesting to note that, unlike in Iceland and Scotland and perhaps the entire rest of the world, where different birds' habitats are separated horizontally, here, on these rocky islands in the choppy North Atlantic, their territories were divided vertically.

Our afternoon fading fast, we took a quick trip around to the other side of the island, where we spotted a small colony of barnacle geese, plus a few eiders and purple sandpipers on the wet rocks near the waterline. To this day I am astonished by the variety of birds we saw in such a small area, and how quickly time passed as we took it all in. By the time we returned to the Explorer it was already approaching dinner hour. We raised anchor and chatted at our tables and made our steady way toward the fjords of Turner Sound.

Bloated with ice, the waters here along the Blosseville Coast posed a navigational hazard – bad enough, at least, for the captain to close off the bridge for a while. Apparently he didn't need any goofballs checking their GPS readings up there while he was trying to keep the boat from sinking.

A trip to the Arctic just wouldn't seem right with the warm sun shining all the time. This is what I told myself as I stood on deck the next morning, staring into a thick swirling mist, shoulders hunched against the cold. Three cups of coffee did little to fend off the elements; we had only time and hope on our side – and not a whole lot of either.

The mercury sat at two degrees above zero, but few of us were about to spend any precious remaining hours cowering from the weather. So once again we formed three groups and took turns jumping into our zodiacs.

From the water and on land we observed countless more birds making the Blosseville coast their temporary home. We also noticed that the vegetation along the coastline was sparser than in the interior of Scoresby. (With the clouds still hanging low and thick there wasn't much else to gawk at.) We bent over to examine the hexagonal patterns in the ground at our feet – true to my suspicions, these were permafrost formations, a common sight on flat areas of land. More intriguing (if that could be possible) were the permafrost dynamics on slightly sloping ground; the melting ice carries along small stones as it flows downhill, forming a loose network of inverted stone gutters. The shoreline was littered with pieces of driftwood and large chunks of ice, left behind like refuse by the tempestuous Arctic waters. As I gazed out at the ocean imagining the Arctic at her worst, the clouds behind me broke, exposing for one shining moment the highest peaks in the Blosseville area.

I'd barely gotten my camera out when they became engulfed in the weather once more.

Back on the ship it was lunch with a view as we sailed a circuit around Turner Ø and up through Rømer Fjord. On the shore steam rose from hot springs; around the vents the arctic vegetation was noticeably extremely rich. On land for a closer look we found thick patches of fern, sticky-leaved, carnivorous butterwort, and purple and blue-white eyebright. We climbed a small hill to an overflowing meter-wide spring. The fifty-degree water spilled out over a short wall of mineral deposits that had been built up over many many years, trickling downhill for a few meters before gathering in a small pool, irresistible to most of our group as a chance to soak our feet.

Boots back on, we discovered a small spring bubbling away at the shoreline. A closer look and we spotted another spring half-submerged in the shallow water – which we then realized was just one more of an entire chain of springs arcing out into the tide. In several places clusters of tiny bubbles on the surface gave away the presence of the springs underwater; in a few spots rocky vesicles peeked up out of the water. In a few years, or a hundred or a thousand, how might these modest geological wonders transform Rømer Fjord? I'd happily come back as a musk ox or even a kittiwake in my next life if it meant I could be around to find out.

Along the shore we found a narwhal skull; this in itself was the greatest discovery of the trip for most of us. Our whale guy Michael just took it in his hands and turned it around, wholly intrigued by the asymmetry in the skull, something of course none of us had noticed. We also found several other bones, also whale as Michael confirmed. Were these, I wondered, leftovers from man or the elements or the scavengers of the land? I picked up a small fragment of bone and toyed with the idea of slipping it into my pocket before returning it to the water.

Our original itinerary called for one more day sailing the coast of Greenland. But the ice was coating the shore like a thick layer of icing on cake; getting anywhere near land would be all but impossible. Thus we would make an overnight crossing of the Straits of Denmark, and we'd spend our last day sailing along the western fjords of Iceland.

Rømer Fjord was the last place we would be standing on Greenlandic soil – and as fitting a spot as any to bid this enchanting island good-bye. Dark, almost black mountains, laced on this day in clouds and mist; hot springs and lush green vegetation, giving the land a very active face; waters boasting colors seldom seen in nature; these are the things we see in the scapes of Greenland. These are the fruits of God's garden.

Our journey to this green land was ending in a markedly beautiful way, underscored with the quiet evidence of how forbidding this land can be. As our ship moved away from the shores of what I decided at that moment was the most beautiful fjord I have ever seen (a sentiment that surfaces time and again in Greenland yet never loses its oomph), my thoughts danced to a song with the apropos title 'Time to Say Goodbye.'

In the evening we were told to gather for a special presentation. We were given no indication as to what it would be about; we were only to pay strict attention. Our collective curiosity grew when Chris, one of the crew members, took the floor before us. Then we sat forward in our chairs as he told us three incredible stories.

George Tyson was the assistant navigator on the Polaris Expedition of 1871, an ill-fated endeavor to sail to the North Pole. On the return trip of this unsuccessful venture the Polaris collided with a low-lying iceberg and began taking on water. Some of the men took to casting cargo overboard to mitigate the progression of the damage; George Tyson and eighteen of the ship's men were separated from the ship when the ice floe they were standing on broke away. The men floated helplessly for six months on the Arctic waters before finally being rescued. Having with them over eight hundred kilograms of food and two skilled Inuit hunters played a fair part, no doubt, in their ultimate survival.

In August 1907 a man named Frederick Cook set out for the North Pole. He returned the following April stating he had reached his goal – a claim that is disputed to this day. Less challenged is Cook's assertion of having spent that summer and most of the arctic winter with his colleagues on Devon Island in Canada's Baffin Bay. Cook and his men were relegated to killing musk ox with stones for food; on one night they literally had to bury themselves in their earthman when a polar bear decided to drop in on them. Fortunately the narrow entrance kept their visitor outside until he finally lost interest. When the frigid winter at long last ended the lingering open water conditions of the previous seasons, Cook's men were able to resume their foot-journey homeward.

Captain Robert Bartlett spent fifty years exploring and mapping the waters of the Far North. He also led over forty expeditions into the Arctic, more than any other person in the history of seafaring. After accompanying Robert Peary on his attempts to reach the North Pole, Bartlett made his own assault in his ice-breaking ship the *Roosevelt*. Though he fell short of his goal, he did make it through to within 130 miles of the

North Pole, and was the first person to sail north of the 88th parallel.

Having told his tales, Chris then asked us to vote for the toughest, most courageous man among the three. The result was not surprising; George Tyson and his colleagues took the crown handily. We wondered aloud what tensions must have arisen among them, how they must have hunted, and simply how they spent their time, sitting there, stuck on an ice floe in far-below-freezing temperatures for half a year. In second place came the eternally-controversial Frederick Cook. Only those with an extreme affinity for sailing rough and high seas voted for their adopted hero Captain Robert Bartlett.

That night, as if Bartlett's ghost were pissed about coming in last, we were all given a taste of what sailing the rough sea meant. Under dark skies the wind strengthened and the waves kicked up, giving all seventy meters of our little red ship *'a bloody good rocking'* as a few of my fellow explorers put it. In the morning, at a weather-delayed breakfast, I asked Thor if we should expect more waves around Iceland. *'Yeah,'* he said, smiling. *'Right up to five meters.'*

I went back to my cabin and plowed through my bags for any stowaway Dramamine.

Relief crept in, ever so slightly, as we gathered for the day's first lecture. Thor explained to us the recent history of the monitoring of ice off the north coast of Iceland. In the first part of the last century large masses of pack ice extended along the entire coast, a forgotten natural phenomenon now as the ice has largely retreated during the last seventy years. We were also introduced to the potential consequences of the decrease of floating ice in the Arctic due to climate change – including, ironically, new commercial sea routes which would likely open.

In the afternoon the weather began to clear, and the seas and my stomach quieted. Our ornithologist Roger explained to us in a short, speedy lecture not only why birds migrate, but also how remarkable these innate instincts and abilities really are. Michael wound things up with a brief talk on the three types of whales that live in the Arctic year round: bowhead, beluga and narwhal. Listening to Michael speak brought an amazing sense of déjà vu, his words conjuring up memories of the first book I ever bought about the Arctic, 'The World of the Arctic Whales,' and the last book I would read before making this pilgrimage to Scoresby Sund. Images of these whales – magical, mysterious and larger-than-life – swam through my head like a living dream.

Then slowly, they faded and disappeared.

I stared at the cement platform of Bruck an der Mur Station as it slowly passed by beneath my window. My mind was awash in memories; none of them seemed quite real. Soon we'd be crossing into Slovenia. Another few hours and I'd be home, taking apart the physical aspects of my journey and putting them away.

The end of the platform appeared and disappeared before my eyes, and in the crushed rocks between the rail lines I spotted a discarded plastic bottle, its label faded from its time in the hot summer sun.

In 2001 I'd dreamt of stumbling upon some undiscovered Viking ruins. After chasing hares and horses and losing mountains I found myself literally walking right into my own little piece of Arctic history. In 2002, inspired by my own fortunate experiences, I decided to try to seek out the remains of the life of the ancient Inuit. After my master Ammassalik plan broke down right along with my burner I walked into the majesty of the Sermilik Ice Fjord. And for as long as I'd known that Greenland existed I wanted to see Scoresby Sund and the grand existence of the Stauning Alps. Through a curious turn of events and three trips to this land I was finally able to venture into these majestic fjords, to witness these beautiful, desolate mountains and complete the journey of my dreams.

In the beginning it was I who decided to set off for that mystical world 'way up there.' Along the winding path chance and circumstance certainly had their say. And in a combination of events I could never have predicted I found myself standing on the ruins, staring at the mountains, soaking up the unspeakable beauty of the paradise of my dreams. Now, as thoughts of Lindenow creep back into my head, I can not help but wonder: has my long, wandering journey of coincidence played itself out? Or is there still such a thing as destiny?

I almost never dream...yet I feel I am living the ongoing pursuit of a deep, deep dream.

A dream called Greenland.

AND FINALLY...

Tidbits of advice for trekking in Greenland

Kalaallit Nunaat is a beautiful, magical place. Don't miss it by choosing a path that is too difficult or demanding for your personal capabilities. How do you choose the proper path? Simple. Do your homework. Read up on existing routes and trails; buy a couple of reliable maps and get to know them; inquire with the local tourist offices in Greenland before you set out, and continue to consult with them as you go. Know your abilities and set a comfortable daily rhythm, whether 5 or 25 kilometers per day. Allow for time to visit ruins, explore surprises and just absorb the place and the time you find yourself in.

Keep in mind there are places suitable for use as a sort of base to avoid having to endure strenuous multi-day hikes. Adequate accommodation can sometimes be found in a shepherd's hut; under benevolent skies, you need no more than your own tent.

The alpha and omega of moving through unfamiliar ground is knowledge in the use of map and compass. In clear weather there is safety and comfort in observing your surroundings. But when the fog descends, when the clouds open up, knowing where you are and which way to go is crucial. Only then can you be reasonably sure you will reach your destination safely. Practice makes perfect, so it is a good idea to get used to using a map and compass at home. Know too what other equipment you will need, and understand how to use it properly, even if you are traveling in an experienced group. You may be called upon to help in dire circumstances. If you are planning to travel in a group, communicate ahead of time who will provide what common equipment and thus lighten everyone's load.

12 recommendations for trekking

(Note that I call these recommendations and not rules; I have a hard enough time following my own advice as it is.)

1. Your trek should suit your level of physical and mental readiness. Don't walk off without adequate training and route planning.

2. Always inform the local tourist office of your travel route. Tell them where you expect to be and when you expect to return.

3. Weather is a key factor out in the wild. Pay attention to forecasts and, if possible, check a few different sources and compare. Then keep your own eye on the ever-changing skies. When bad conditions loom, caution is a key factor of survival. Do not challenge the weather. Mother Nature can be kind, but she never loses.

4. Listen to the advice of experienced trekkers.

5. Be prepared for bad weather and accidents by noting shorter routes.

6. Never forget your map and compass – and know how to use them!

7. Never trek alone. (Good one, Damjan.)

8. Swallow your pride and retreat before a situation becomes critical.

9. Save enough time and energy to properly set up camp.

10. Always carry a basic first aid kit.

11. Always keep your warm clothes with you, even on shorter routes.

12. Never allow your sleeping bag to get wet. A dry sleeping bag is a key factor of physical (and most assuredly mental) survival in the wild.

Some positive thoughts for the end

• In the Arctic, as in life, encountering difficulties and problems is inevitable. Identifying and correcting them before they overwhelm is up to us.

• From time to time the fog sets in. If we know where we are and where we are going we can still move toward our goal, even when we can't see ten meters in front of us. Then when the fog finally lifts may we find ourselves closer than ever to our destination.

• We are all human. We all have limits. Push yours toward your chosen horizon. Just don't step blindly over them.

• Outside of life's routine, in the face of the fierce whims of circumstance, we come to better understand the soul residing within us. How we react to the moment is the cause, not the effect, of who we truly are.

• The way is not always marked. The power of the journey lies in creating a path where there is none.

• Hurdling the obstacles and barriers in our way, we change more than our physical location.

• There is beauty in chasing your dreams. There is beauty in experiencing the moment. There is no greater beauty than when these two become one.

• Eventually, we all come face to face with an ice cold river. Here begins the struggle for our survival, when we show ourselves how we want to live.

CPSIA information can be obtained
at www.ICGtesting.com
Printed in the USA
BVOW09s1942160817
492240BV00013B/89/P